ALGEBRA 1 RESCUE!

Student Book
Chapters 1–6

SOPRIS
WEST
EDUCATIONAL SERVICES

ISBN 1-57035-935-0

Developmental editing by Sandy Rusch
Copy editing by Beverly Rokes
Editorial assistance by Annette Reaves
Text layout by Kathy Bone and Sopris West
Cover design by Maria Coccaro
Production assistance by Scott Harmon

07 06 05 04 03   6 5 4 3 2 1

Printed in the United States of America

Published and Distributed by

SOPRIS
WEST
EDUCATIONAL SERVICES

4093 Specialty Place • Longmont, CO 80504
(303) 651-2829 • www.sopriswest.com

169ALG/169STBK1-6/5-02/BAN/15M/133

Contents

Chapter 1 Variables and Expressions. 1-1

Chapter 2 Exploring Rational Numbers. 2-1

Chapter 3 Solving Linear Equations 3-1

Chapter 4 Graphing Relations and Functions. 4-1

Chapter 5 Analyzing Linear Equations 5-1

Chapter 6 Solving Linear Inequalities. 6-1

Glossary. G-1

Pretest

Write a *mathematical* expression for each written expression.

1. The product of nine and twelve reduced by sixteen

2. Eight squared minus the quantity of four times six

3. Seven increased by the product of thirteen and the number x

4. Ten multiplied by the quantity x plus seven

5. The product of two and the square of x

Write a *verbal* expression for each mathematical expression.

6. $7 + (9 \times 3)$

7. $(14 + 24) \times (7 - 2)$

8. $x^2 - 17$

9. $(2y)^2$

10. $2 \times 17 - 5$

Worksheet 1

Write the equivalent mathematical expression for the given verbal expression.

<u>Problem</u>   <u>Answer</u>

1. seven plus three   1. _____

2. six subtracted from nine   2. _____

3. the product of two and seven   3. _____

4. ten increased by seven   4. _____

5. five plus two times nine   5. _____

6. four times seven minus twenty   6. _____

7. five times the quantity three plus one   7. _____

8. x increased by three   8. _____

9. six subtracted from y   9. _____

10. the product of two and a   10. _____

11. x added to seven   11. _____

12. five plus two times y   12. _____

13. four times x minus twenty   13. _____

14. five times the quantity x plus one   14. _____

15. the quantity x plus four multiplied by 8   15. _____

16. the sum of seven and nine times x   16. _____

17. the quantity of x minus two times the quantity of x plus one   17. _____

18. six plus four times x minus seventeen   18. _____

Worksheet 2

Write the equivalent verbal expression for the given mathematical expression.

Problem   Verbal Expression

1. $7 + 8$ 1. _____

2. $2x$ 2. _____

3. $2 \times 3 + 1$ 3. _____

4. $3 \times 6 - 1$ 4. _____

5. $5x - 4$ 5. _____

6. $3x^2$ 6. _____

7. $3(x + 1)^2$ 7. _____

8. $2^2 - 4$ 8. _____

9. $(x + 2)^2$ 9. _____

10. $x + 2^2$ 10. _____

11. $5x - 9$ 11. _____

12. $x^2 + y^2$ 12. _____

13. $(x + y)^2$ 13. _____

14. $7x^2 + 2x + 3$ 14. _____

15. $3x^2 + 4y - 5$ 15. _____

Worksheet 3

Fill in the missing equivalent verbal or mathematical expressions. Answers may vary.

Equivalent Verbal Expression	Equivalent Mathematical Expression
1. thirteen increased by the factors two and two	1. _____
2. _____	2. $(5 + 2^3)2 - 5$
3. five percent of seven percent of thirteen	3. _____
4. _____	4. $7(3) - 4$
5. the product of nine and seven, the quantity squared	5. _____
6. _____	6. $3^2 - 17(-2)$
7. the difference between the sum of seven and nine and the sum of nine and eleven	7. _____
8. _____	8. $(5 - 7)2$
9. fifty-two thousandths times nine and ninety-eight hundredths dollars	9. _____
10. _____	10. $(7.5\%)(\$1.95)$
11. the product of three and seven increased by nine	11. _____
12. _____	12. $3(7 + 9)$
13. two cubed minus seven squared	13. _____
14. two cubed minus seven, the quantity squared	14. _____

Algebra 1 Rescue! ©2004 Sopris West Educational Services. To order: 800-547-6747. Product Code 169ALG

Posttest

Write a *mathematical* expression for each written expression.

1. Six times the quantity of nine minus six

2. The sum of eight squared and the quantity four times eleven

3. Three times x minus seven

4. Nine multiplied by x squared

5. The product of the quantity x plus five and the quantity x minus five

Write a *verbal* expression for each mathematical expression.

6. $(8 + 4) \times 8 + 4$

7. $(4 + 5) \times (2 + 17)$

8. $3(x + 2)$

9. $(x + 2)^2$

10. $3x + 5$

Pretest

Find the value of each mathematical expression.

1. $17 - 6 \times 2 + (4 + 7) =$ ___

2. $3 \times 7 - 8 + 4 \times 3 =$ ___

3. $(5 \times 2 - 1)4 =$ ___

4. $3^2 - 2 \times 2 =$ ___

5. $(3 + 1)^2 - 7 =$ ___

Find the value of each algebraic expression if a = 4 and b = 3.

6. $(a + 4)(b - 1) =$ ___

7. $7 + ab - a =$ ___

8. $(a + b)a - b =$ ___

9. $(a + b)(a - b) =$ ___

10. $b^a =$ ___

Algebra 1 Rescue! ©2004 Sopris West Educational Services. To order: 800-547-6747. Product Code 169ALG

Worksheet 1

I. Evaluate the following expressions by using the order of operations. [*Example:* $11 - 2 \times 3 = 5$]

1. $3 \times 6 - 2 =$ ___

2. $5^2 + 9 =$ ___

3. $5 + 4 \times 6 =$ ___

4. $18 - 7 \times 2 + 7 =$ ___

5. $3 \times 6 + 9 \times 4 =$ ___

6. $8 + 3 + 6 \times 2 =$ ___

7. $17 - 3 \times 5 =$ ___

8. $28 - 6 \times 4 + 5 =$ ___

9. $9 \times 3 + 9 \times 7 =$ ___

10. $3.6 \times 4 - 6.2 =$ ___

II. Evaluate the following expressions. [*Example:* $(2 \times 3) + 9 = 15$]

1. $7 + (2 \times 6) =$ ___

2. $(9 - 4) + (4 \times 3) =$ ___

3. $15 - 7 + (6 \times 2) =$ ___

4. $6 \times (7 - 4) + 12 =$ ___

5. $(3 + 7) \times (9 - 3) =$ ___

6. $7 + (12 - 4) - 2 =$ ___

7. $35 \times (17 - 7) + 13 =$ ___

8. $40 - 11 \times 3 =$ ___

9. $42 - 6 \times 2 + 7 =$ ___

10. $14 + 3 \times (6 - 4) =$ ___

11. $3.8 \times 4 - 1.6 =$ ___

12. $\frac{2}{3} + \left(\frac{1}{2} - \frac{1}{6}\right) =$ ___

Worksheet 2

Evaluate each expression by using the order of operations.
[*Example:* $6 \times (7 - 3) + 4 = 6 \times 4 + 4 = 24 + 4 = 28$]

1. $11 - 4 \times 2 = $ _____

2. $(15 - 4) \times 6 = $ _____

3. $3 + 12 - 3^2 = $ _____

4. $8^2 - (4 \times 8) = $ _____

5. $8 + 4 \times 3 - 5 = $ _____

6. $27 - (6 + 8) = $ _____

7. $(3 + 8)(9 - 4) = $ _____

8. $6 \times (4 - 2) + 5 = $ _____

9. $8^2 + 2 \times 5 - 8 = $ _____

10. $(3 + 7)^2 = $ _____

11. $(6 + 3)(6 - 3) = $ _____

12. $4 + (7 - 2)^2 + 3 = $ _____

13. $(6 + 3)^2 - (6 - 3)^2 = $ _____

14. $8 \times (11 - 7) \times (3 + 4) = $ _____

15. $3^2 + 17 - 4 \times 3 = $ _____

16. $8 + 4^2 - 3^2 = $ _____

Algebra 1 Rescue! ©2004 Sopris West Educational Services. To order: 800-547-6747. Product Code 169ALG

Worksheet 3

I. Find the value of each expression if x = 2, y = 6, and z = 4. [*Example:* (x + y)z = (2 + 6)4 = 32]

1. xy = ___

2. 2x + y = ___

3. 6 + xz = ___

4. xy − z = ___

5. 6x − 2z = ___

6. 4 + x(y − z) = ___

7. $\frac{1}{2}$(2x + z) = ___

8. xyz = ___

9. (6 + x)x − z = ___

10. $x^2 + y^2$ = ___

II. Find the value of each expression if a = 3, b = 6, and c = 4. [*Example:* 2b − 4 = 2 × 6 − 4 = 8]

1. 8 − 2a = ___

2. 16 − a^2 + c = ___

3. ab − 4 = ___

4. 7 − b ÷ a + c = ___

5. b − 2a + 7 = ___

6. 3b − 4c = ___

7. $\frac{b + 3c}{a}$ = ___

8. $(a + c)^2$ = ___

9. a + b + c − 2a = ___

10. (b − c) × a = ___

11. 0.5b + c − a = ___

12. 3(b − a) + 12 = ___

Algebra 1 Rescue! ©2004 Sopris West Educational Services. To order: 800-547-6747. Product Code 169ALG

Worksheet 4

Write the missing verbal expression or mathematical expression and find the solutions.

Verbal Expression	Mathematical Expression
1. thirteen increased by the product of two and two	1. _____
2. _____ _____	2. $(5 + 2^3)2 - 5$
3. five percent of ten times thirteen	3. _____
4. _____ _____	4. $7(3) - 4$
5. the product of nine and seven, the quantity squared	5. _____
6. _____ _____	6. $22 + 5 \times 4 + 1$
7. the difference between the sum of seven and nine and the sum of nine and eleven	7. _____
8. _____ _____	8. $(5 - 7)2$
9. fifty-two thousandths times nine and ninety-eight hundredths dollars	9. _____
10. _____ _____	10. $(3 + 5) \times 7 - 12$
11. three times seven increased by nine	11. _____
12. _____ _____	12. $3(7 + 9)$
13. the quantity three plus five times eight	13. _____
14. two minus seven, the quantity squared	14. _____

Posttest

Find the value of each mathematical expression.

1. $7 + (11 - 6) \times 8 =$

2. $14 - 3^2 + 5 \times 4 =$

3. $17 - 2^3 + 4 =$

4. $5 + 2 \times 3 - 7 =$

5. $[(5 + 2) - 3]4 =$

6. $(9 - 3)^2 + 7 \times 3 =$

Find the value of each algebraic expression if a = 6 and b = 3.

7. $a + 3b - 2a =$

8. $(a - 2)(b + 2) =$

9. $[(a + 2b) - 10] \times 2 =$

10. $(a + b)^2 =$

Pretest

1. For the equation $2x + 3 = 17$, which number makes the equation true: $x = 3$, $x = 5$, or $x = 7$?

2. $2(y - 3) = 6$. If $y = 4$, is the equation true or false?

3. $c = 2d - 17$. Find c if $d = 13$.

4. Find x if $x = \dfrac{13 + 4 \times 3}{5}$.

5. $x = 2^y$. Find x if $y = 3$.

6. For the equation $x + 3 + 9x = 8x + 23$, which number makes the equation true: $x = 10$, $x = 2$, or $x = 7$?

7. If $z = 4$, is the equation $z(z + 2) = 5^2$ true or false?

8. For the equation $y = 2x^2 + 3x - 7$, find y when $x = 3$.

9. For the equation $a = (b + c)^2 - 25$, find a when $b = 2$ and $c = 3$.

10. What is the value of x if $x = \frac{1}{2} + \frac{2}{3}\left(\frac{3}{4}\right)$?

Algebra 1 Rescue! ©2004 Sopris West Educational Services. To order: 800-547-6747. Product Code 169ALG

Worksheet 1

Determine if each given statement is True, False, or Open.

Problem	Statement	True	False	Open
1	It is behind the barn next to the tractor.			
2	In the order of the days of the week, Thursday always comes after Wednesday and before Friday.			
3	When x is added to twenty-seven, the sum can be thirty.			
4	When twenty-seven is added to three, the sum can be forty.			
5	George Washington was the first president of the United States of America.			
6	He lived in South Carolina.			
7	For any real number x, x > 5.			
8	For any real number x, x + 5 = 22.			
9	For any real number x, if x = 7, then x + 5 = 12.			
10	$2(5 + 4) - 7 = 7$			
11	$3(4 - 3) + 6 = 9$			
12	For any real number called x, $3(x + 5) = 3x + 15$.			
13	For any real number called x, $5(x + 7) = 5x + 12$.			
14	$[2 + 6(9 - 7)2^2]3 + 3 = 51$			
15	$[2 + 6(9 - 7)2^2]3 + 3 = 153$			
16	Now is the time for a man to come to the aid of his country.			
17	Tom Cruise is a movie star.			
18	He starred in more than five movies.			
19	Tom is not married.			

Algebra 1 Rescue! ©2004 Sopris West Educational Services. To order: 800-547-6747. Product Code 169ALG

Worksheet 2

Label the statement as True, False, or Open when each of the values is used for the variable.

Problem	Statement	x = 2	x = 3	x = 5
1	William Jefferson Clinton had x terms as president of the United States of America.			
2	x − 3 = x − 3			
3	x + 5 = x + 7			
4	x + 7 = 2x + 5			
5	3(x + 2) = 3x + 6			
6	McDonald's is an American fast-food restaurant with x golden arches in the company logo.			
7	There are exactly x of these McDonald's restaurants in Colorado.			
8	x − 5 = 0			
9	TV programs can be received on channel x in this city.			
10	x + 7 < 2x + 9			
11	x(1/x) = 1			
12	x + x + x = 0			
13	(x − 5)(2x) = 0			
14	A triangle has x sides.			
15	$3^x = 27$			
16	3x + 18 = 11x + 2			
17	2x − 7 = x + 2			
18	x subtracted from 13 is 8.			
19	The product of the quantities x + 2 and x − 2 is zero.			

Algebra 1 Rescue! ©2004 Sopris West Educational Services. To order: 800-547-6747. Product Code 169ALG

Worksheet 3

Find the value for each formula. [*Example:* P = 2l + 2w; l = 14 feet, w = 8 feet.
Solution: P = 2(14) + 2(8) = 44 feet.]

1. $A = \frac{1}{2}(b_1 + b_2) \times h$ $b_1 = 9, b_2 = 11, h = 6$ A = _____

2. $y = x^2 + 3x + 1$ $x = 4$ y = _____

3. $V = \pi r^2 h$ $\pi = 3.14, r = 6, h = 5$ V = _____

4. $C = \frac{5}{9}(F - 32)$ $F = 77$ C = _____

5. $y = \frac{a^2 + b^2}{a - b}$ $a = 6, b = 1$ y = _____

6. $y = (x + 3)^2$ $x = 5$ y = _____

7. $P = (5\%)(3)(400)$ P = _____

8. $y = 2x + 6 - x$ $x = 11$ y = _____

Posttest

1. For the equation $3(x - 4) = 18$, which number makes the equation true: $x = 5$, $x = 10$, or $x = 15$?

2. $4(y + 2) - 6 = 14$. If $y = 3$, is the equation true or false?

3. $A = 6b + 5$. Find A if $b = 4$.

4. Find x if $x = \dfrac{(8 + 2) \times 3}{6}$.

5. For the equation $3x^2 + 2x - 9 = 7$, which number makes the equation true: $x = 1$, $x = 2$, or $x = 3$?

6. Find x if $x = \dfrac{2 + 3 \times 4}{7}$.

7. When $c = d^2 - 9$, find c when $d = 4$.

8. If $y = 2$, is the equation $y^2 + y = 9$ true or false?

9. Find a when $b = 3$ and $c = 4$ for $a = (b + 3)^2 \div 4$.

10. When $x = 3$, is the equation $2x + y = 6$ true, false, or open?

Algebra 1 Rescue! ©2004 Sopris West Educational Services. To order: 800-547-6747. Product Code 169ALG

Pretest

Evaluate the following mathematical expressions by using the properties to make the computation as easy as possible.

1. $25 + (134 + 75) =$ _____

2. $(18 \times 7) \times (13 \times 0) =$ _____

3. $(17 \times 8) + (17 \times 2) =$ _____

4. $\left[\frac{5}{6}(2 + 7)\right] \times \frac{6}{5} =$ _____

5. $5 \times 17 \times 20 =$ _____

6. $\frac{3 + 7}{4} \times \frac{4}{10} =$ _____

7. $123 \times 4 =$ _____

8. $[3(4 + 5) + 2] \times 0 =$ _____

9. $(4 - 2)(13 + 1) \times 1 =$ _____

10. $9(2 + 3) =$ _____

Algebra 1 Rescue! ©2004 Sopris West Educational Services. To order: 800-547-6747. Product Code 169ALG

Worksheet 1

Rewrite each mathematical expression so it will be easy to compute, then compute the answer.

[*Example:* $(5 \times 53) \times 20 = (5 \times 20) \times 53 = 100 \times 53 = 5{,}300$]

1. $(16 + 37) + 4 =$

2. $\frac{3}{4} \times \left(\frac{2}{5} \times \frac{4}{3}\right) =$

3. $35 + 22 + 5 + 8 =$

4. $47 \times 69 \times 0 \times 97 =$

5. $(14 \times 7) + (14 \times 3) =$

6. $(17 + 8) \times (5 + 5) =$

7. $4 \times (51 \times 25) =$

8. $2.4 + 7.7 + 5.6 + 0.3 =$

9. $\frac{3}{4} \times (17 \times 4) =$

10. $\frac{5}{8} + \left(\frac{2}{9} + \frac{3}{8}\right) =$

11. $(9 \times 67) \times (12 \times 0) =$

12. $(6 + 17) + (4 + 3) =$

13. $(2 \times 8) \times 5 =$

14. $\frac{3}{8} \times \left(15 \times \frac{8}{3}\right) =$

15. $17 + (83 + 68) =$

Algebra 1 Rescue! ©2004 Sopris West Educational Services. To order: 800-547-6747. Product Code 169ALG

Worksheet 2

Compute the answers to the problems below by using properties to make the computation easier. Name one property you used.

<u>Problem</u>   <u>Property Used</u>

1. $(15 \times 7) \times 0 =$ 1. _____

2. $\frac{5}{8} \times \left(19 \times \frac{8}{5}\right) =$ 2. _____

3. $(47 + 3) + (-3) =$ 3. _____

4. $(8 \times 7) + (8 \times 3) =$ 4. _____

5. $20 + 7.4 + 80 =$ 5. _____

6. $(29 + 17) + (13 + 21) =$ 6. _____

7. $25 \times (17 - 6) \times 4 =$ 7. _____

8. $40 \times (11 \times 5) =$ 8. _____

9. $\frac{5}{6} + \left(\frac{1}{7} + \frac{1}{6}\right) =$ 9. _____

10. $(16 \times 7) \times (12 \times 0) =$ 10. _____

11. $9 + 7 + 3 + 8 + 1 + 2 =$ 11. _____

12. $5 \times (37 \times 2) =$ 12. _____

13. $5 \times 40 \times 1 =$ 13. _____

14. $44 + 17 + 56 + 83 =$ 14. _____

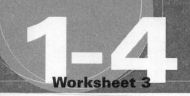

Worksheet 3

Each of the following equalities illustrates a mathematical property. Name the property.

<u>Equality</u>   <u>Mathematical Property Name</u>

1. $(x + 2) + 0 = (x + 2)$ 1. _____

2. $(\$4.98)1 = \$4.98$ 2. _____

3. $(7x)9 = 7(x9)$ 3. _____

4. $(589\%)(0) = 0$ 4. _____

5. $\left(\frac{x+2}{9}\right)\left(\frac{9}{x+2}\right)$, when $x \neq -2$ 5. _____

6. $3(x^2 + 2x - 7) = (x^2 + 2x + 7)3$ 6. _____

7. $(x + 5)(x + 9) = (x + 5)x + (x + 5)9$ 7. _____

8. $(x + 7) + 5 = x + (7 + 5)$ 8. _____

9. $x + (7 + 5) = (7 + 5) + x$ 9. _____

10. $29(x + 4) = (x + 4)29$ 10. _____

11. $(x - 5)x = x(x - 5)$ 11. _____

12. $x(x + 9) = x^2 + x9$ 12. _____

Algebra 1 Rescue! ©2004 Sopris West Educational Services. To order: 800-547-6747. Product Code 169ALG

Worksheet 3 (continued)

Each of the following equalities is the result of applying more than one mathematical property. Name, in order, all of the mathematical properties used to transform the left-hand side of the equality into the right-hand side of the equality.

Equality   Mathematical Properties Required

13. $x(x + 7) = x^2 + 7x$

1. _____

2. _____

14. $5 + x(x + 2) = x^2 + 2x + 5$

1. _____

2. _____

3. _____

15. $(5 - 5)\left(\frac{1}{2}\right) = 0$

1. _____

2. _____

3. _____

16. $x(2x + 3x + 7 + 2) = 5x^2 + 9x$

1. _____

2. _____

3. _____

4. _____

Algebra 1 Rescue! ©2004 Sopris West Educational Services. To order: 800-547-6747. Product Code 169ALG

Posttest

Evaluate the following mathematical expressions by using the properties to make the computation as easy as possible.

1. $40 + (217 + 60) =$

2. $8 \times (9 \times 3) \times 0 =$

3. $(14 \times 7) + (14 \times 3) =$

4. $\left[\frac{1}{4} \times (5 + 12)\right] \times 4 =$

5. $10 \times 132 =$

6. $(5 \times 9) + (5 \times 11) =$

7. $\frac{1}{17}(9 + 8) =$

8. $7(3.14159) + 3(3.14159) =$

9. $5\%(81) + 5\%(19) =$

10. $13(100 + 20 + 5) =$

Algebra 1 Rescue! ©2004 Sopris West Educational Services. To order: 800-547-6747. Product Code 169ALG

Chapter 1 Test — Variables and Expressions

Objective 1-1

Write a mathematical expression for each written expression:

1. The sum of nine and five times seven

    _____

2. The product of eleven and x squared

    _____

Write a verbal expression for each mathematical expression:

3. $(4 + 8) - (6 - 3)$ _____

4. $25 - 8 \times (4 - 2)$ _____

Objective 1-2

5. $8 \times 3 - 6 + 3 \times 4 =$ _____   6. $9 \times (4 + 3) - (5 \times 7) =$ _____

7. $3 + 6^2 \div 9 =$ _____   8. Evaluate $3 \times (a - b) + 7$ when $a = 5$ and $b = 3$. _____

Objective 1-3

9. Find p if $p = 2l + 2w$ and $l = 8$ and $w = 7$.

    _____

10. For the equation $3x - 4 = 8$, which number makes the
    equation true: $x = 2$, $x = 3$, $x = 4$, or $x = 5$?

    _____

11. True or false: $3x + 16 = 37$ if $x = 5$?

    _____

12. Find x if $x = \dfrac{19 - 2^2}{3}$.

    _____

Objective 1-4

Evaluate the following mathematical expressions by using properties to make the computation as easy as possible.

13. $(25 \times 19) \times 4 =$ _____   14. $\frac{5}{7} \times \left(11 \times \frac{7}{5}\right) =$ _____

15. $700 + (483 + 300) =$ _____   16. $(9 + 32) \times (8 - 5) \times 0 =$ _____

Algebra 1 Rescue! ©2004 Sopris West Educational Services. To order: 800-547-6747. Product Code 169ALG

Pretest

Graph each set of numbers on the number line.

1. {Integers less than zero}

2. $\left\{-2\frac{1}{2}, -1, 0, 1, 2\frac{1}{2}\right\}$

3. {−3, −1, 3}

4. {Integers greater than −2}

5. {2, −7, 7, −5, 9}

6. {Integers between 3 and −3}

7. {−.9, .5, 1, −.25}

8. {Integers less than −2}

9. $\left\{2\frac{1}{2}, -3, 4\frac{3}{4}, -\frac{1}{2}\right\}$

10. {50, −10, 0, 25, −40}

Algebra 1 Rescue! ©2004 Sopris West Educational Services. To order: 800-547-6747. Product Code 169ALG

Worksheet 1

A. *(Example: Answer to #1)*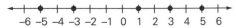

1. Using number line A, put a dot on the following rational numbers: –3, 1, 5, –5, and 3.

2. How many numbers did you graph? _____

3. Is the set finite or infinite? _____

4. Express the numbers as a set: _____

B.
   -6 -5 -4 -3 -2 -1 0 1 2 3 4 5 6

5. Using number line B, graph this set of numbers: {–4, –3, –2, –1, . . .}.

6. How many integers did you graph? _____

7. Does the graphed set of numbers *stop* or *continue on indefinitely*? _____

8. Is the graphed set an *infinite* set or a *finite* set? _____

C.
   -6 -5 -4 -3 -2 -1 0 1 2 3 4 5 6

9. Using number line C, graph this set of numbers: {–6, –4.9, –3½, –1.75, 0, ½, 2, 3.4, 5}.

D.
   -6 -5 -4 -3 -2 -1 0 1 2 3 4 5 6

10. Using number line D, graph this set of numbers: {Integers between –5 and 6}.

Algebra 1 Rescue! ©2004 Sopris West Educational Services. To order: 800-547-6747. Product Code 169ALG

Worksheet 2

Graph the following sets on the given number lines.

1. *(Example)* {–3, –1, 0, 2, 3}

2. {–2, 1, 2, 3}

3. {–7, 4, 9, 0, –3}

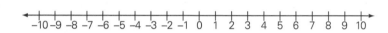

4. {–2.5, –0.5, 1.5, 2.8}

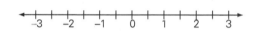

5. $\left\{-8, -1\frac{1}{2}, 5\frac{1}{2}, -6\frac{3}{4}, 8\right\}$

6. {Integers between –3 and 3}

7. {Integers greater than –2}

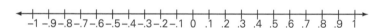

8. {Integers less than 2}

9. {.6, –.2, .25, –.4, .9}

Write in set notation the sets that are graphed in problems 10–16.

10. _____

11. _____

12. _____

13. _____

14. _____

15. _____

16. _____

Worksheet 3

Label the number lines so you can graph each set. Then graph the following sets on the given number lines.

1. *(Example)* {Integers between −4 and +4}

    -5 -4 -3 -2 -1 0 1 2 3 4 5

2. {Integers less than 12}

3. {Integers greater than −30}

4. {−3, 0, 3, 4}

5. {−400, −100, 0, 200, 300}

6. {−2$\frac{1}{2}$, −$\frac{4}{5}$, 0, 1.8, 2.5}

7. {Even integers from −4 to +4}

8. {Odd integers from −3 to +3}

9. {$\frac{1}{2}$, 1, −.7, −.1, $\frac{3}{4}$}

10. {Negative integers}

11. {Integers}

12. {−2$\frac{1}{2}$, −1$\frac{1}{2}$, 0, 1$\frac{1}{2}$, 2$\frac{1}{2}$}

13. {−0.4, −0.2, 0, 0.1, 0.3}

14. {Even nonpositive integers}

15. {−20, 10, 30, −10, 5}

Posttest

Graph each set of numbers on the number line.

1. {Integers less than 2}

2. {Integers between 4 and −4}

3. $\left\{-3\frac{1}{2}, -1\frac{1}{3}, 1, 2\frac{1}{2}, 3.7\right\}$

4. {−4, 2, −2, 3}

5. {−8, 3, −2, 9, 6}

6. {Integers greater than 0}

7. {−.7, .2, −.1, .5}

8. {Integers less than 4}

9. $\left\{-3, 1\frac{1}{2}, 3.5, -1\right\}$

10. {60, −20, 0, −15, 79}

Pretest

Simplify:

1. $-3 + (-2) =$ _____

2. $-3 + 5 =$ _____

3. $0 - 3 =$ _____

4. $3 + (-5) =$ _____

5. $-3 - 7 =$ _____

6. $-8 + 0 =$ _____

7. $-3 + 7 =$ _____

8. $-0.3 + 0.5 =$ _____

9. $-\frac{1}{3} - \frac{1}{2} =$ _____

10. $0.34 - 0.52 =$ _____

Worksheet 1

Evaluate the following problems as in the example.

(*Example*) +8 + (−3) = (+5)   =   +5

1. −4 + (+6) = _____

2. +9 + (−5) = _____

3. −9 + (+5) = _____

4. −9 + (−5) = _____

5. −8 + (+8) = _____

6. +8 + (−3) = _____

7. −6 + (−12) = _____

8. +38 + (−17) = _____

9. −16 + (−4) = _____

10. −14 + (−7) = _____

11. −4 + (+14) = _____

12. +11 + (−16) = _____

13. +14 + (−18) = _____

14. +6 + (−12) = _____

15. 0 + (+11) = _____

16. −14 − (+11) = _____

17. +11 − (−14) = _____

18. −17 + (+12) = _____

19. +5 + (+28) = _____

20. −234 + (+188) = _____

21. +1,246 − (+1,418) = _____

Algebra 1 Rescue! ©2004 Sopris West Educational Services. To order: 800-547-6747. Product Code 169ALG

Worksheet 2

I. Study the two examples (problems 1 and 2), then complete the remainder of the subtraction problems.

1. *(Example)* $+4 - (-3) = 4 + (+3) = 7$

2. *(Example)* $-5 - (-2) = -5 + (+2) = -3$

3. $-3 - (-5)$ $= -3 + (+5)$ $=$ _____

4. $-3 - (+5)$ $= -3 +$ _____ $=$ _____

5. $15 - (-15)$ $=$ _____ $=$ _____

6. $-15 - (-15)$ $=$ _____ $=$ _____

7. $-15 - (+15)$ $=$ _____ $=$ _____

8. $15 - (+15)$ $=$ _____ $=$ _____

9. $25 - (-11)$ $=$ _____ $=$ _____

10. $-25 - (-11)$ $=$ _____ $=$ _____

11. $-25 - (+11) =$ _____ $=$ _____

12. $25 - (+11)$ $=$ _____ $=$ _____

13. $13 - (-12)$ $=$ _____ $=$ _____

14. $-13 - (-12) =$ _____ $=$ _____

15. $-13 - (+12) =$ _____ $=$ _____

II. Perform these additions and subtractions.

16. $-11 + (-12) =$ _____

17. $-12 - (+20) =$ _____

18. $12 + (-37) =$ _____

19. $3.7 + (-5.4) =$ _____

20. $-3.7 - (-5.4) =$ _____

21. $3.7 - (+5.4) =$ _____

22. $4\frac{1}{4} + \left(-2\frac{1}{2}\right) =$ _____

23. $-3\frac{1}{2} - \left(-2\frac{1}{2}\right) =$ _____

24. $+7 - \left(-2\frac{1}{2}\right) =$ _____

Algebra 1 Rescue! ©2004 Sopris West Educational Services. To order: 800-547-6747. Product Code 169ALG

Worksheet 3

Use the number lines to find the answers to the following problems.

(*Example*) 6 + (–3) = +3

   1. +4 + (+5) = _____

   2. +4 + (–2) = _____

   3. –6 + (+4) = _____

   4. +6 – (+2) = _____

   5. +8 – (+6) = _____

   6. –10 + (+12) = _____

   7. –3 – (+4) = _____

   8. +5 – (+5) = _____

   9. +7 – (–3) = _____

  10. –3 – (–4) = _____

  11. –8 – (–5) = _____

  12. +6 – (–2) = _____

  13. +2 – (+6) = _____

  14. +9 + (–13) = _____

  15. +4 + (–8) = _____

Algebra 1 Rescue! ©2004 Sopris West Educational Services. To order: 800-547-6747. Product Code 169ALG

Worksheet 4

Find the solutions to the following addition and subtraction problems.

1. *(Example)* +7 + (−5) = +2

2. +6 + (+9) = _____

3. −8 + (−4) = _____

4. +6 − (+8) = _____

5. +3 − (−3) = _____

6. −6 − (+4) = _____

7. +11 − (+8) = _____

8. −4 − (−12) = _____

9. −3 − (+6) = _____

10. +13 + (−10) = _____

11. −4 + (+10) = _____

12. −7 + (+7) = _____

13. +2 + (−9) = _____

14. +3 − (−10) = _____

15. +16 + (−8) = _____

16. +67 + (+18) = _____

17. −61 + (−12) = _____

18. −24 + (+55) = _____

19. −13 − (−21) = _____

20. +12 − (−3.5) = _____

21. $-1\frac{1}{2} + (+17) =$ _____

22. $-2\frac{1}{4} + \left(+6\frac{1}{2}\right) =$ _____

23. −12.35 − (−13.22) = _____

24. +100 − (+14.3) = _____

Posttest

Simplify:

1. $-5 + (-4) = $ _____

2. $-5 + 14 = $ _____

3. $-1 - 1 = $ _____

4. $5 + (-14) = $ _____

5. $-15 + 7 = $ _____

6. $-3 + 0 = $ _____

7. $-15 - 7 = $ _____

8. $\frac{2}{5} - \frac{1}{2} = $ _____

9. $-0.4 + 0.5 = $ _____

10. $-0.35 + (-0.28) = $ _____

Pretest

1. Arrange the following numbers in order from the smallest to the largest:
   1, −3, 0, −2, 2, −4, −5.

2. Arrange the following numbers in order from the smallest to the largest:
   −8, 4, −3, 8, −5, 13.

3. Arrange the following numbers in order from the smallest to the largest:
   −5, 7, −1, 1, 3, −10.

4. Arrange the following numbers in order from the smallest to the largest:
   $-\frac{1}{2}$, .9, −.3, .31, −.9, $-\frac{3}{4}$.

Place the symbol <, >, or = between each pair of numbers to make the sentence true.

5. −3 ___ 10

6. −3.1 ___ −4

7. $+\frac{3}{4}$ ___ $+\frac{4}{5}$

8. .31 ___ .2

9. −.31 ___ −.2

10. −21 ___ −22

Worksheet 1

1. Graph these integers on the given number line: 5, 0, –3, –1, –2, 4, 3.

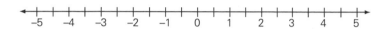

2. Rank the numbers in problem 1 from smallest to largest.

3. Place the inequality symbol > or < between each pair of numbers to make a true sentence:

   a. 5 ____ 0   b. 0 ____ –3   c. –3 ____ –1

   d. –1 ____ –2   e. –2 ____ 4   f. 4 ____ 3

4. Place these low temperatures on the number line below.

January 1	–10°	January 2	–12°
January 3	–2°	January 4	5°
January 5	12°	January 6	16°

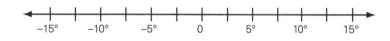

5. Rank the low temperatures from problem 4 from smallest (or coldest) to largest (or warmest).

Algebra 1 Rescue! ©2004 Sopris West Educational Services. To order: 800-547-6747. Product Code 169ALG

Worksheet 2

Rearrange the following numbers from smallest to largest:

1. −5, 5, 10, −10, 9, −9, −3   _____, _____, _____, _____, _____, _____

2. 3, 2, 0, −2, −3, 1   _____, _____, _____, _____, _____, _____

3. 1, −3, 5, −5, 3, −1   _____, _____, _____, _____, _____, _____

4. −100, −101, −99, +99, 100, −98   _____, _____, _____, _____, _____, _____

5. $-1\frac{1}{2}$, $1\frac{1}{2}$, 2, 1, −2, −1, 0   _____, _____, _____, _____, _____, _____

Place the symbol <, >, or = between the numbers to make a true statement.

6. −1 ____ 1

7. −1 ____ 0

8. −1 ____ −2

9. −1 ____ $-1\frac{1}{2}$

10. −1 ____ $-\frac{1}{2}$

11. −1 ____ −1.1

12. −13 ____ −12

13. −13 ____ −14

14. .13 ____ 13.1

15. −.13 ____ −13.1

16. −4 ____ −3

17. 4 ____ 3

18. 14 ____ 13

19. −14 ____ −13

20. −1 ____ 100

Algebra 1 Rescue! ©2004 Sopris West Educational Services. To order: 800-547-6747. Product Code 169ALG

Worksheet 3

Rearrange the following numbers from smallest to largest:

1. $-3, 5, -4, 4, -5$ _____, _____, _____, _____, _____

2. $-\frac{1}{2}, \frac{2}{3}, -\frac{1}{4}, \frac{1}{2}$ _____, _____, _____, _____

3. $0.3, -0.1, -0.2, 0.2$ _____, _____, _____, _____

4. $-4, \frac{21}{5}, -3.95, -\frac{15}{4}$ _____, _____, _____, _____

5. $0, -\frac{5}{5}, \frac{5}{5}, -\frac{10}{5}, \frac{10}{5}$ _____, _____, _____, _____, _____

Place the symbol <, >, or = between the numbers to make a true statement (calculator may be used).

6. -4 ____ $-\frac{15}{4}$ 7. -3.95 ____ -4 8. 0 ____ -1

9. 4 ____ $\frac{16}{4}$ 10. $-\frac{1}{2}$ ____ $-\frac{1}{4}$ 11. $\frac{1}{2}$ ____ $\frac{1}{4}$

12. -3 ____ -4 13. 0.30 ____ 0.4 14. $\frac{1}{4}$ ____ -10

15. $-\frac{1}{4}$ ____ -0.2 16. $\frac{1}{4}$ ____ 0.2 17. 0 ____ $-\frac{1}{4}$

18. $-\frac{1}{4}$ ____ $-\frac{4}{16}$ 19. $\frac{5}{16}$ ____ $\frac{3}{8}$ 20. $-\frac{1}{2}$ ____ $-\frac{7}{16}$

21. Place these profits or losses on the number line below: loss of $10.50, profit of $5.75, loss of $7.25, loss of $6.75, profit of $4.50.

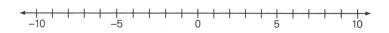

22. Rank the five numbers in problem 21 from smallest to largest.

23. Was the total of all five numbers a profit or a loss? Of how much? (Express as a rational number.)

Algebra 1 Rescue! ©2004 Sopris West Educational Services. To order: 800-547-6747. Product Code 169ALG

Posttest

1. Arrange the following numbers in order from the smallest to the largest: –1, 1, –1.5, –3, 3.

2. Arrange the following numbers in order from the smallest to the largest: –7, 4, –5, 2, –9, 3.

3. Arrange the following numbers in order from the smallest to the largest: –1, 3, –2, 2, –3, –4.

4. Arrange the following numbers in order from the smallest to the largest:
   $-.1, -.27, \frac{1}{2}, .6, -.7, .51$.

Place the symbol <, >, or = between each pair of numbers to make the sentence true.

5. –1 ___ 7

6. $+1\frac{1}{2}$ ___ $-2\frac{3}{5}$

7. 3.8 ___ 2.9

8. –3 ___ –3.1

9. –.84 ___ –.9

10. –.9 ___ –.91

Pretest

Simplify:

1. $(-5) \times (2) =$ _____

2. $\frac{-15}{-3} =$ _____

3. $-5 \times (-13) =$ _____

4. $7 \times (-13) =$ _____

5. $-12 \times (-5) =$ _____

6. $-60 \div (-5) =$ _____

7. $\frac{60}{-12} =$ _____

8. $-48 \div 12 =$ _____

9. $-5.2 \times (-3.1) =$ _____

10. $\left(\frac{3}{4}\right) \div \left(-\frac{9}{10}\right) =$ _____

Worksheet 1

Find the product for each problem.

(Example) $+7 \times (-8) = -56$

1. $+6 \times (+9) = $ _____

2. $+8 \times (-4) = $ _____

3. $+8 \times (-11) = $ _____

4. $-2 \times (+16) = $ _____

5. $-6 \times (-9) = $ _____

6. $-4 \times (-7) = $ _____

7. $+3 \times (-7) = $ _____

8. $+11 \times (+5) = $ _____

9. $+11 \times (-10) = $ _____

10. $+7 \times (-9) = $ _____

11. $-5 \times (+5) = $ _____

12. $-6 \times (-4) = $ _____

13. $+7 \times (-12) = $ _____

14. $-9 \times (-12) = $ _____

15. $+8 \times (+8) = $ _____

16. $-10 \times (+10) = $ _____

17. $+12 \times (-12) = $ _____

18. $+6 \times (-0.5) = $ _____

19. $+\frac{1}{2} \times \left(-\frac{1}{4}\right) = $ _____

20. $+3 \times (-9) = $ _____

21. $+16 \times (-7) = $ _____

22. $+8 \times (-12) = $ _____

23. $-9 \times (-13) = $ _____

24. $[11 \times (-9)] \times \left(-\frac{1}{3}\right) = $ _____

Algebra 1 Rescue! ©2004 Sopris West Educational Services. To order: 800-547-6747. Product Code 169ALG

Worksheet 2

Find the quotient for each problem.

(*Examples*) $-16 \div (-4) = 4$ $\qquad$ $-16 \div \frac{4}{3} = \left(\frac{-16}{1}\right) \times \frac{3}{4} = -12$

1. $+6 \div (+3) =$ _____

2. $+6 \div (-2) =$ _____

3. $-18 \div (+6) =$ _____

4. $-24 \div (-3) =$ _____

5. $+21 \div (+7) =$ _____

6. $+24 \div (-6) =$ _____

7. $-25 \div (-5) =$ _____

8. $+16 \div (-4) =$ _____

9. $-32 \div (-4) =$ _____

10. $-72 \div (+9) =$ _____

11. $+40 \div (-8) =$ _____

12. $+18 \div (+9) =$ _____

13. $-77 \div (+11) =$ _____

14. $-42 \div (+6) =$ _____

15. $-132 \div (-12) =$ _____

16. $-12 \div (-6) =$ _____

17. $-294 \div (+7) =$ _____

18. $-45 \div (-9) =$ _____

19. $-17 \div (+2) =$ _____

20. $-330 \div (-6) =$ _____

21. $+\frac{1}{2} \div \left(-\frac{1}{2}\right) =$ _____

22. $+12.5 \div (-5) =$ _____

23. $15 \div (-3) =$ _____

24. $-15 \div \left(-\frac{1}{3}\right) =$ _____

Worksheet 3

Simplify:

(Examples) $\frac{^-45}{15} = -3$ $-15 \times (-3) = 45$

1. $-3 \times (-4) =$ _____

2. $-3 \times 4 =$ _____

3. $-5 \times 6 =$ _____

4. $-5 \times (-6) =$ _____

5. $-20 \div 4 =$ _____

6. $20 \div (-5) =$ _____

7. $30 \div (-6) =$ _____

8. $-30 \div (-5) =$ _____

9. $9 \times (-8) =$ _____

10. $-9 \times (-8) =$ _____

11. $-12 \times (-9) =$ _____

12. $12 \times (-11) =$ _____

13. $-150 \div 15 =$ _____

14. $-150 \div (-10) =$ _____

15. $\frac{60}{-15} =$ _____

16. $\frac{-60}{-6} =$ _____

17. $-5 \times (-3 \times 2) =$ _____

18. $5 \times [-4 \times (-3)] =$ _____

19. $-6 \times [24 \div (-3)] =$ _____

20. $-5 \times (-35 \div 7) =$ _____

21. $24 \div [-1 \times (-3)] =$ _____

22. $-24 \div (-2 \times 4) =$ _____

Worksheet 4

Multiply: *(Example)* $-8 \times (-3) = 24$

1. $4 \times (-30) = $ _____
2. $-4 \times (-30) = $ _____
3. $-15 \times 12 = $ _____

4. $-15 \times (-12) = $ _____
5. $15 \times (-12) \times (-2) = $ _____
6. $(-4)(-2)(3) = $ _____

7. $(-7)(-5) = $ _____
8. $(-9)(17) = $ _____

9. $\left(2\frac{3}{4}\right)\left(-3\frac{4}{5}\right) = $ _____
10. $(-3.17)(-2.4) = $ _____

If $a = -4$, find: *(Example)* $3a = 3(-4) = -12$

11. $2a = $ _____
12. $-3a = $ _____
13. $(4a)(-2a) = $ _____

Divide: *(Example)* $\frac{-40}{-5} = 8$

14. $(-120) \div (-20) = $ _____
15. $\frac{-120}{30} = $ _____
16. $48 \div (-12) = $ _____

17. $-48 \div (-8) = $ _____
18. $-480 \div 30 = $ _____
19. $\frac{-30 - 5}{-7} = $ _____

20. $(-30 + 5) \div (-5) = $ _____

If $a = 4$, find: *(Example)* $\frac{-5a}{2} = \frac{-5(4)}{2} = \frac{-20}{2} = -10$

21. $\frac{6a}{-8} = $ _____
22. $\frac{-2a + 5a}{-12} = $ _____
23. $\frac{3a - 4}{8} = $ _____

Simplify: *(Example)* $(-3 \times 15) \div (-9) = -45 \div (-9) = 5$

24. $\frac{56}{-7} = $ _____
25. $(-11)(-9) = $ _____
26. $(13)(-1)(-2) = $ _____

27. $\frac{-144}{9} = $ _____
28. $(-144) \div (-16) = $ _____
29. $(-120)\left(\frac{3}{4}\right) = $ _____

30. $(-12) \div \left(-\frac{3}{4}\right) = $ _____

Posttest

Simplify:

1. $(-4) \times (13) =$ _____

2. $\frac{-28}{-7} =$ _____

3. $-96 \div (-6) =$ _____

4. $-8 \times (-12) =$ _____

5. $-5 \times (-14) =$ _____

6. $-84 \div 12 =$ _____

7. $\frac{80}{-16} =$ _____

8. $16 \times (-6) =$ _____

9. $-4.3 \times (-3.7) =$ _____

10. $\left(-\frac{3}{5}\right) \div \left(\frac{1}{15}\right) =$ _____

Pretest

Find the following square roots. Calculators may be used. Round to the nearest $\frac{1}{100}$ when the expression is irrational.

1. $\sqrt{9} =$ _____

2. $\pm\sqrt{81} =$ _____

3. $\sqrt{49} =$ _____

4. $-\sqrt{36} =$ _____

5. $-\sqrt{100} =$ _____

6. $\sqrt{400} =$ _____

7. $\pm\sqrt{900} =$ _____

8. $\sqrt{45} =$ _____

9. $\sqrt{21} =$ _____

10. $\sqrt{140} =$ _____

Worksheet 1

Fill in the blanks to make true statements.

(*Example*) Since (3)(3) = 9, **9** is the **square** of 3, and **3** is the square root of __9__ .

1. Since (4)(4) = 16, _____ is the _____ of 4, and _____ is the _____ of 16.

2. Since (6)(6) = 36, _____ is the _____ of _____, and 6 is the _____ of 36.

3. Since $(7)^2$ = 49, 49 is the _____ of _____, and 7 is the square root of _____.

4. Since $(9)^2$ = _____, _____ is the square of _____, and 9 is the square root of _____.

5. Since $\frac{1}{4} \times \frac{1}{4} = \frac{1}{16}$, $\frac{1}{16}$ is the square of _____, and _____ is the square root of _____.

6. Since (.5)(.5) = _____, _____ is the square of .5, and .5 is the square root of _____.

7. Since $\left(\frac{2}{3}\right)^2 = \frac{4}{9}$, $\frac{4}{9}$ is the _____ of $\frac{2}{3}$, and _____ is the square root of _____.

8. Since $(2.5)^2$ = _____, _____ is the square of 2.5, and 2.5 is the square root of _____.

9. Write a similar statement involving 20 and $(20)^2$.

10. Write another statement involving any number and its square.

Worksheet 2

1.
   • • •
   • • •
   • • •
   The diagram shows that _____ is the square of _____, and _____ is the square root of _____.

2.
   • • • •
   • • • •
   • • • •
   • • • •
   The diagram shows that _____ is the square of _____, and _____ is the square root of _____.

3.
   • • • • • •
   • • • • • •
   • • • • • •
   • • • • • •
   • • • • • •
   • • • • • •
   The diagram shows that _____ is the square of _____, and _____ is the square root of _____.

4. $5 \times 5 = 5^2 =$ _____

5. $\sqrt{25} =$ _____

6. $(9)(9) = 9^2 =$ _____

7. $\sqrt{81} =$ _____

8. $(12)(12) = (12)^2 =$ _____

9. $\sqrt{144} =$ _____

10. $\frac{5}{6} \times \frac{5}{6} = \left(\frac{5}{6}\right)^2 =$ _____

11. $\sqrt{\frac{25}{36}} =$ _____

12. $\left(\frac{1}{7}\right)^2 =$ _____

13. $\sqrt{\frac{1}{49}} =$ _____

14. $(-11)(-11) =$ _____

15. $-\sqrt{121} =$ _____

16. $(-15)^2 =$ _____

17. $-\sqrt{.49} =$ _____

18. $(1.5)^2 =$ _____

19. $\pm\sqrt{100} =$ _____

20. $\left(\frac{6}{7}\right)^2 =$ _____

21. $\sqrt{\frac{121}{144}} =$ _____

22. $(8)^2 =$ _____

23. $\sqrt{64} =$ _____

Worksheet 3

Simplify the following expressions. Estimate to the nearest $\frac{1}{100}$ when the expression is irrational. Use calculators only when you have to.

1. $3^2 =$ _____

2. $5^2 =$ _____

3. $7^2 =$ _____

4. $\sqrt{25} =$ _____

5. $\sqrt{9} =$ _____

6. $\sqrt{49} =$ _____

7. $6^2 =$ _____

8. $13^2 =$ _____

9. $15^2 =$ _____

10. $\sqrt{220} =$ _____

11. $\sqrt{30} =$ _____

12. $\sqrt{169} =$ _____

13. $-\sqrt{25} =$ _____

14. $\pm\sqrt{169} =$ _____

15. $\sqrt{\frac{25}{169}} =$ _____

16. $\sqrt{1.21} =$ _____

17. $-\sqrt{.49} =$ _____

18. $\pm\sqrt{1.44} =$ _____

19. $\sqrt{45} =$ _____

20. $-\sqrt{3} =$ _____

21. $\sqrt{7} =$ _____

22. $\sqrt{64} =$ _____

23. $\sqrt{12} =$ _____

24. $\pm\sqrt{600} =$ _____

25. $\sqrt{100} =$ _____

26. $-\sqrt{4,900} =$ _____

27. $\sqrt{77} =$ _____

28. $\sqrt{2} =$ _____

29. $\sqrt{32} =$ _____

30. $\pm\sqrt{8} =$ _____

Posttest

Find the following square roots:

1. $\sqrt{121} =$ _____

2. $\sqrt{16} =$ _____

3. $\pm\sqrt{49} =$ _____

4. $-\sqrt{16} =$ _____

5. $\sqrt{225} =$ _____

6. $-\sqrt{36} =$ _____

7. $\pm\sqrt{1,600} =$ _____

Use a calculator to find the square root to the nearest $\frac{1}{100}$.

8. $\sqrt{35} =$ _____

9. $\sqrt{70} =$ _____

10. $\sqrt{200} =$ _____

Chapter 2 Test—Exploring Rational Numbers

Objective 2-1

Graph the following sets of numbers:

1. {−3, 7, −1, 2}

2. $\{\frac{3}{4}, -.5, .1, -\frac{2}{3}\}$

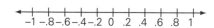

3. {Integers greater than −3}

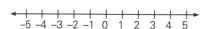

4. {25, −10, 5, −30}

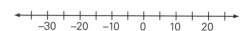

Objective 2-2

Find the solutions:

5. −8 + (−13) = ____   6. 5 − (−4) = ____   7. −27 − 17 = ____   8. 3.7 + (−5.2) = ____

Objective 2-3

Place the symbol >, <, or = in the blank to make the sentence true:

9. 10 ___ −10   10. −3.2 ___ 3.1   11. 22 ___ 22.5

12. Arrange the following set of numbers in order from smallest to largest:
     {6, −11, $3\frac{1}{2}$, −4, 14, −5.5}.

Objective 2-4

Find the solutions:

13. −12 × (+7) = ____   14. −18 ÷ 3 = ____   15. −5 × (−19) = ____   16. −36 ÷ (−12) = ____

Objective 2-5

Find the square roots of the following. Use a calculator and estimate the answer to the nearest $\frac{1}{100}$.

17. $\sqrt{49}$ = ____   18. $\sqrt{72}$ = ____   19. $-\sqrt{81}$ = ____   20. $\pm\sqrt{20}$ = ____

Pretest

Solve the following equations.

1. $6 + y = 6$

2. $3 = 7 + x$

3. $x + 27 = -24$

4. $y + (-5) = 12$

5. $m - 18 = -13$

6. $-13 + t = -27$

7. $50 - g = 47$

8. $28 + m = -39$

9. $.75 + d = -.5$

10. $x - 1\frac{1}{4} = 2\frac{1}{2}$

Worksheet 1

Solve each equation and check the answer.

Example: x + 7 = 16	
x + 7 − 7 = 16 − 7	
x = 9	
Check: **9 + 7 = 16**	

1. x − 2 = 8

2. 3 + x = 6

3. x + 11 = 1

4. 2 + x = 12

5. x − 3 = 14

6. 4 + x − 10 = 14

7. 6 + x = 14

8. 32 + x = 12

9. x + 13 = −4

10. 4 = x − 7

11. 7 − x = 4

12. 4 + x = 2x

13. x − 16 = 17 + 13

14. 104 + x = 212

15. x + 7 = 0

16. 6 − x = −9

17. 27 + x = 10

18. 2 = 12 + x

19. x − 14 = −6

20. 12 = x − 7

Algebra 1 Rescue! ©2004 Sopris West Educational Services. To order: 800-547-6747. Product Code 169ALG

Worksheet 2

Solve each equation and check the answer.

Example: $\quad 3.2 = 1.4 + x$	1. $a = -19 - 17$
$3.2 - 1.4 = 1.4 - 1.4 + x$	
$1.8 = x$	
Check: $\quad 3.2 = 1.4 + 1.8$	
$3.2 = 3.2$	

2. $a + 19 = -17$

3. $a + 17 = -19$

4. $x = 28 + (-47)$

5. $47 = 28 + x$

6. $-28 = -47 - x$

7. $-15 + d = -22$

8. $4.8 = 13.9 + m$

9. $-7 = -19 + (-k)$

10. $\frac{1}{6} + 2m = \frac{2}{3}$

11. $t + (-9) = 18$

12. $g - 37 = 49$

13. $-142 = m + 217$

14. $s - 13.5 = -9.1$

15. $u - \left(-\frac{7}{8}\right) = \frac{15}{16}$

16. $\$4.18 = t - \$17.97$

17. $.6 = y - .7$

18. $4,987 + d = -7,289$

19. $x - \left(-\frac{27}{18}\right) = \frac{5}{9}$

20. $4\frac{3}{5} + y = 7.2$

Posttest

Solve the following equations.

1. $x + 4 = 9$

2. $y - 3 = 2$

3. $t + (-13) = 27$

4. $-13 = m + 18$

5. $12 = y + 5$

6. $24 = x - 27$

7. $59 - x = 147$

8. $3 + y = -11$

9. $1.8 + x = 4.2$

10. $2y + 6 - y = 11$

Pretest

Solve the following equations.

1. $8x = 16$

2. $5y = -15$

3. $\frac{t}{3} = 7$

4. $\left(-\frac{1}{2}\right)x = 4$

5. $\frac{3}{4}x = 9$

6. $-2x = -28$

7. $\frac{x}{8} = 2$

8. $\frac{1}{3}(x) = -5$

9. $-2x = -18$

10. $-27 = \frac{3}{2}x$

Worksheet 1

Solve each equation and check the answer.

Example: $17x = -34$	
$\frac{1}{17}(17)x = \frac{1}{17}(-34)$	
$x = -2$	
Check: $17(-2) = -34$	

1. $4x = 12$

2. $-3y = 18$

3. $75 = 5x$

4. $-146 = 2y$

5. $3n = -210$

6. $7x = \frac{3}{4}$

7. $7.5x = 1.5$

8. $.8y = 3.20$

9. $-8.8 = 2.2x$

10. $5x = 480\left(\frac{1}{2}\right)$

11. $18x = 36$

12. $6x = -120$

13. $-9x = -72$

14. $-76 = 4x$

15. $16y = -8$

16. $18x = 45$

17. $3.2x = .32$

18. $.04x = (.3)(.4)$

19. $0x = 120$

20. $-2 = 6x$

Worksheet 2

Solve each equation and check the answer.

Example:	$\frac{1}{2}x = 10$
	$2\left(\frac{1}{2}\right)x = 2(10)$
	$x = 20$
Check:	$\frac{1}{2}(20) = 10$
	$10 = 10$

1. $\frac{1}{3}x = -5$

2. $\frac{x}{3} = -5$

3. $-\frac{1}{7}x = 4$

4. $-\frac{x}{7} = 4$

5. $\frac{y}{-7} = 2$

6. $\frac{y}{4} = \frac{5}{6}$

7. $\frac{6m}{5} = -6$

8. $\frac{1}{5}(6n) = -6$

9. $\frac{x}{4} = 22$

10. $-40 = \frac{8}{5}b$

11. $\frac{x}{4} = 54$

12. $\frac{1}{2x} = -5$

13. $6x = -18$

14. $4y = -28$

15. $\frac{3x}{4} = 9$

16. $\frac{1}{8}(3x) = 6$

17. $x \div 7 = 106$

18. $-\frac{1}{2}x = -14$

19. $x \cdot \frac{3}{4} = -24$

20. $3x + 8 = 29$

Algebra 1 Rescue! ©2004 Sopris West Educational Services. To order: 800-547-6747. Product Code 169ALG

Posttest

Solve the following multiplication and division problems for the variables.

1. $17x = 85$

2. $3x = -69$

3. $\frac{1}{6}x = 9$

4. $\frac{x}{4} = 27$

5. $-\frac{1}{8}x = 3$

6. $\frac{x}{3} = 7$

7. $-11x = 18.7$

8. $\left(\frac{2}{5}\right)x = 16$

9. $-27x = 27$

10. $\frac{3}{4}x = \frac{9}{36}$

Pretest

Solve the following equations.

1. $3 + x = 6$

2. $x + 13 = 1$

3. $5x - 2 = 33$

4. $-14 = 5x + 1$

5. $\frac{x - 2}{3} = -12$

6. $\frac{1}{3}x + 4 = 7$

7. $-1 = 5 + 6x$

8. $2x + 3 = x + 2$

9. $\frac{1}{2}x + 6 = 8$

10. $3x + 7 = x - 5$

Worksheet 1

Solve each equation and check the answer.

Example: $2x + 4 = 9$ **Check:** $2\left(\frac{5}{2}\right) + 4 = 9$
$2x = 5$ $2\left(\frac{1}{2}\right)(5) + 4 = 9$
$x = \frac{5}{2}$ or $2\frac{1}{2}$ $5 + 4 = 9$
$9 = 9$

1. $9x - 8x = 14$

2. $21y + (-13) - 20y = 8$

3. $21y - 20y + (-13) = 8$

4. $21y - 20y = 8 + 13$

5. $21y - 20y = 21$

6. $13t + (-12)t = 3.14$

7. $13t + (-12t) = 12t + (-12t) + 3.14$

8. $13t = 12t + 3.14$

9. $-32 = 17a - 16a$

10. $4y = 28$

11. $4y - 2y = 8$

12. $2x + 3 = 17$

13. $11 = 2y + 1$

14. $4x + 2 = 0$

15. $2 - 3x = 8$

16. $-19 = 3x + (-7)$

17. $9 - 2x = 3$

18. $73 = 8x + 9$

19. $2x + 15 = 5x - 33$

20. $y + 12(y - 2) = 4y - 27$

Algebra 1 Rescue! ©2004 Sopris West Educational Services. To order: 800-547-6747. Product Code 169ALG

Worksheet 2

Solve the equations in the following rows. Check your answers. Once you see a relation between columns, state what the relation is, and you can shortcut the activity by solving only the equations in the right-hand column. Explain, in your own words, what rules were applied in moving from Column 1 to Column 2 and from Column 2 to Column 3.

Column 1	Column 2	Column 3	Solutions
$5n - 9 = 71$	$5n = 71 + 9$	$5n = 80$	
$4d + 9 = -3$	$4d = -3 - 9$	$4d = -12$	
$3y - 4 = 14$	$3y = 14 + 4$	$3y = 18$	
$2x - 1 = 11$	$2x = 12$	$\frac{1}{2}(2x) = \frac{1}{2}(12)$	
$3p + 8 = -16$	$3p = -24$	$\left(\frac{1}{3}\right)(3p) = \frac{1}{3}(-24)$	
$-2x + 5 = 19$	$-2x = 14$	$\left(-\frac{1}{2}\right)(-2x) = \left(-\frac{1}{2}\right)(14)$	
$5n = 80$	$\frac{1}{5}(5n) = \frac{1}{5}(80)$		
$\frac{x}{2} = 15$	$2\left(\frac{x}{2}\right) = 2(15)$		
$\frac{1}{7}y = -3$	$7\left(\frac{1}{7}y\right) = (7)(-3)$		
$\frac{a}{8} = \frac{3}{4}$	$8\left(\frac{a}{8}\right) = 8\left(\frac{3}{4}\right)$		
$\frac{2 + m}{7} = -3$	$7\left(\frac{2 + m}{7}\right) = (7)(-3)$	$2 + m = -21$	
$-\frac{2}{3}(2y + 4) = 8$	$-\frac{3}{2}\left(-\frac{2}{3}\right)(2y + 4) = \left(-\frac{3}{2}\right)8$	$2y + 4 = -12$	
$7 = \frac{15 + 9x}{6}$	$(6)(7) = 6\left(\frac{15 + 9x}{6}\right)$	$42 = 90 + 9x$	

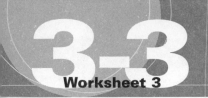

Worksheet 3

Solve each equation and check the answer.

Example: $7x - 3 = 4x + 15$	**Check:** $7(6) - 3 = 4(6) + 15$
$7x - 4x - 3 = 4x - 4x + 15$	$42 - 3 = 24 + 15$
$3x - 3 + 3 = 15 + 3$	$39 = 39$
$3x = 18$	
$x = 6$	

1. $2x - 9 = 3 - x$

2. $4x + 5 = 2x + 7$

3. $4x + 12 = x + 3$

4. $2(x - 5) = 12$

5. $24 = 4(y - 3)$

6. $\frac{1}{2}(28) = 2(3 + 2n)$

7. $7x + 4 = 9x + 24 - 2x$

8. $3y + 9 = 4y + 15$

9. $4x + 1 = 7x - 17$

10. $-6x + 9 = -4x - 3$

11. $-3y - 8 = -5y + 12$

12. $t - 7 = 3\frac{1}{2} + 2t$

13. $2x - 20 = 20$

14. $3x + 5 = -7$

15. $4x + 8 = 3x$

16. $7x = -2x + 18$

17. $-3x + 24 = 2x - 1$

18. $5(m - 5) = 45$

19. $5p - 3p - 30 = -18$

20. $3x - 40 = x - 18$

Algebra 1 Rescue! ©2004 Sopris West Educational Services. To order: 800-547-6747. Product Code 169ALG

Worksheet 4

Solve each equation and check the answer.

Example: $\frac{1}{2}$(x + 3) = x + 2   **Check:** $\frac{1}{2}$(–1 + 3) = –1 + 2

$$2\left(\tfrac{1}{2}\right)(x + 3) = 2(x + 2) \qquad\qquad \tfrac{1}{2}(2) = 1$$

$$x + 3 = 2x + 4 \qquad\qquad\qquad 1 = 1$$

$$x + 3 - 4 = 2x + 4 - 4$$

$$x - 1 - x = 2x - x$$

$$-1 = x$$

1. $\frac{1}{4}$x + $\frac{3}{4}$x = 0 – x

2. 0.7x + 0.3x = 2x – 4

3. x + 2 = $\frac{x}{2}$ – 2

4. 4(x + 2) = 3x

5. 4x + 8 = 3x

6. 2x = 3x + 2

7. –7x = 2x + 18

8. 4x + 5 = 2x + 1

9. 17x + 17 = –17

10. $\frac{x + 4}{3}$ = 8

11. y + 6y = 22 – 4y

12. 1.3 + 9.4x – 9.03x = 3.52

13. $\frac{1}{2}$x + 14 = 30

14. 6x – 7 = 2x + 9

15. 2y + 2 = $\frac{3y}{2}$

16. 0.5x – 3 = 2.25 + 1.5x

17. $\frac{1}{4}$(4x + 12) = x + 3

18. 6x + 19 – 2x = x + 16

19. $\frac{1}{5}$(4x + 3) = 7

Posttest

Solve the following equations.

1. $5 + x = 7$

2. $x + 9 = 2$

3. $5x - 12 = 13$

4. $\frac{1}{3}x = 22$

5. $\frac{x - 4}{5} = 9$

6. $3x - 5 = x + 9$

7. $2 = 2x + 8$

8. $5x - 14 = 2x + 13$

9. $\frac{1}{2}x + 8 = \frac{1}{3}x + 9$

10. $-3x + 4 = 2x + 9$

Algebra 1 Rescue! ©2004 Sopris West Educational Services. To order: 800-547-6747. Product Code 169ALG

Pretest

1. Five times a number is 375. What is that number?

2. One hundred twenty students are going on the New York field trip. This represents one-third of the junior class. How many students are in the junior class?

3. The sum of three consecutive integers is 171. What are the integers?

4. The perimeter of a rectangle is 408 inches. If the length of one side is 70 inches, what is the measure of the other side? (P = 2l + 2w)

5. The three angles of a triangle add to a sum of 180°. If a right triangle has an angle of 63°, what is the measure of the third angle?

Worksheet 1

Write equations for each of the following sentences. Then answer the questions by solving the equations and check your work.

1. The sum of twice a number and 32 is 78. What is the number?

2. Two times a number added to 32 is 78. What is the number?

3. Taking three times a given number, dividing it by two, and adding that result to eight gives the same result as multiplying the number by four and then subtracting the result from 32. What is the number?

4. The decimal 1.4 subtracted from a number is zero. What is the number?

5. An amount of money less $\frac{3}{4}$ of a dollar leaves $\$4\frac{1}{4}$. What was the original amount of money?

6. Find a number that is 96 greater than its opposite.

7. Find a number whose product with 9 is the same as its sum with 56.

8. Find a number that is 68 greater than three times its opposite.

9. Four times a number increased by 25 is 13 less than 6 times the number. Find the number.

10. If twice an integer is the same as one-third of six times that integer, what is the integer?

11. What are three consecutive integers whose sum is 39?

12. Find four consecutive even integers whose sum is −92.

13. Two odd integers differ by 4 and their sum is 226. What are the integers?

14. Five consecutive even integers have a sum of 0. Write an equation you would use to find these integers. Solve the equation and write the five integers.

Algebra 1 Rescue! ©2004 Sopris West Educational Services. To order: 800-547-6747. Product Code 169ALG

Worksheet 2

Write equations for each of the following geometry sentences. Then answer the questions by solving the equations and check your work.

1. A triangle has three angles labeled A, B, and C. If $\angle A$ is 15° and $\angle B$ is 90°, what is the measure of $\angle C$?

2. An isosceles triangle has two angles that measure 50°. What is the measure of the third angle?

3. A right triangle has one angle that measures 52°. What are the measures of the other two angles?

4. An equilateral triangle has three sides that are equal in length and three angles that are equal in measure. What is the measure of each angle of an equilateral triangle?

5. One angle of a triangle is three times the measure of another. If the third angle measures 80°, what are the measures of the other two angles?

6. An obtuse triangle is also isosceles. If the obtuse angle measures 120°, what is the measure of the other two angles?

Given the quadrilateral shown here, find the solution to the following problems if $\angle b = 60°$ and $\angle e = 85°$.

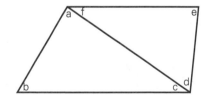

7. If $\angle c$ measures 25°, what is the measure of $\angle a$?

8. Find the measure of $\angle d$ if $\angle f$ measures 17°.

9. If $\angle a + \angle f = 115°$, what is the sum of the measure of $\angle c + \angle d$?

10. If $\angle a + \angle f = 120°$ and $\angle c = 40°$, what is the measure of $\angle d$?

Algebra 1 Rescue! ©2004 Sopris West Educational Services. To order: 800-547-6747. Product Code 169ALG

Posttest

1. Find three consecutive odd integers whose sum is 105.

2. Four more than three times a number is twenty-two. What is that number?

3. If an isosceles triangle has one side that is twice the length of its shortest side, and its perimeter is 65 inches, what are the measurements of its three sides?

4. You and your friends ate three of the eight pizzas ordered. Your combined share of the price for what you ate was $15.75. What was the total bill for the eight pizzas?

5. Given the figure ABCD, what is the measurement of ∠ADC?

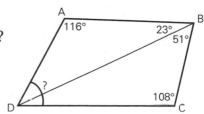

Algebra 1 Rescue! ©2004 Sopris West Educational Services. To order: 800-547-6747. Product Code 169ALG

Pretest

Do the following pairs of ratios form proportions?

1. $\frac{3}{2}, \frac{21}{14}$

2. $\frac{6}{8}, \frac{22}{28}$

Solve the following proportions:

3. $\frac{x}{2} = \frac{9}{6}$

4. $\frac{x}{45} = \frac{3}{15}$

5. $\frac{y}{9} = \frac{-7}{16}$

6. $\frac{x}{3} = \frac{x+3}{15}$

7. $\frac{-3}{x} = \frac{15}{-10}$

8. $\frac{9}{16} = \frac{9}{2x}$

A recipe for bread uses 2 cups of liquid and 6 cups of flour for 3 loaves of bread.

9. How many cups of flour are needed for 10 loaves?

10. How much liquid is needed if 21 cups of flour are used?

Worksheet 1

The comparison of two numbers by division, $\frac{a}{b}$, is a ratio.

The equation formed by two equivalent ratios, $\frac{a}{b} = \frac{c}{d}$, is a proportion.

The cross product, ad = bc, can be shown as being equivalent by using the multiplication principle of equality. That is, if two ratios are equal, $\frac{a}{b} = \frac{c}{d}$, then $(bd)\frac{a}{b} = (bd)\frac{c}{d}$, and ad = bc, where ad and bc are cross products.

Using the cross product, show which of the following pairs of ratios are proportions.

> *Example:* $\quad \frac{1}{4} = \frac{2}{8}$
> $$1 \cdot 8 = 2 \cdot 4$$
> $$8 = 8$$
> **Yes, this is a proportion.**

1. $\frac{1}{2}, \frac{2}{4}$

2. $\frac{4}{7}, \frac{7}{14}$

3. $\frac{3}{8}, \frac{18}{48}$

4. 7:13, 21:39

5. 2.5/6, 5/11

6. 3.7:37, 1:10

Solve the following proportions: *(Example)* $\quad \frac{2}{5} = \frac{x}{20} \qquad 5x = 40 \qquad x = 8$

7. $\frac{x}{5} = \frac{15}{25}$

8. $\frac{4}{7} = \frac{12}{x}$

9. $\frac{9}{4t} = \frac{3}{8}$

10. $\frac{8}{5t} = \frac{2}{5}$

11. $\frac{3}{x} = \frac{15}{60}$

12. $\frac{x}{100} = \frac{49}{7}$

13. $\frac{7}{8} = \frac{x}{40}$

14. $\frac{11}{x} = \frac{132}{24}$

15. $\frac{x}{5} = \frac{14}{20}$

Algebra 1 Rescue! ©2004 Sopris West Educational Services. To order: 800-547-6747. Product Code 169ALG

Worksheet 2

Solve the proportions:

1. $\frac{x}{9} = \frac{2}{3}$

2. $\frac{20}{100} = \frac{4}{x}$

3. $\frac{2}{x} = \frac{1}{15}$

4. $\frac{5}{x} = \frac{1}{5}$

5. $\frac{6}{21} = \frac{x}{7}$

6. $\frac{1}{12} = \frac{10}{x}$

7. $\frac{4}{x} = \frac{2}{9}$

8. $\frac{x}{18} = \frac{5}{6}$

9. $\frac{x}{24} = \frac{2}{3}$

10. $\frac{15}{100} = \frac{3}{x}$

11. $\frac{x}{8} = \frac{2}{20}$

12. $\frac{25}{100} = \frac{x}{32}$

13. $\frac{9}{2} = \frac{3x}{4}$

14. $\frac{8}{x} = \frac{1}{15}$

15. $\frac{x}{6} = \frac{7}{3}$

16. $\frac{3 + 2m}{3 - 2m} = \frac{-3}{1}$

17. $\frac{m}{8} = 2$

18. $\frac{2.5}{4} = \frac{10}{x}$

19. $\frac{x + 2}{4} = \frac{20}{8}$

20. $\frac{1}{x} = \frac{21}{44 - x}$

Algebra 1 Rescue! ©2004 Sopris West Educational Services. To order: 800-547-6747. Product Code 169ALG

Posttest

Do the following pairs of ratios form proportions?

1. $\frac{5}{4}, \frac{75}{60}$

2. $\frac{3}{10}, \frac{7.5}{25}$

3. $\frac{8}{12}, \frac{2}{5}$

Solve the following proportions:

4. $\frac{7}{8} = \frac{x}{100}$

5. $\frac{2}{5} = \frac{x}{35}$

6. $\frac{3}{x} = \frac{4}{28}$

7. $\frac{4}{x+2} = \frac{2}{9}$

8. $\frac{11}{x} = \frac{132}{24}$

9. $\frac{12}{x} = \frac{3}{4}$

10. A 96-mile trip required 6 gallons of gasoline. At the same rate, how many gallons would be required for a 152-mile trip?

Algebra 1 Rescue! ©2004 Sopris West Educational Services. To order: 800-547-6747. Product Code 169ALG

Pretest

1. 25% of _____ is 8.

2. 6% of 1,000 is _____.

3. 30% of 120 is _____.

4. 14 is 10% of _____.

5. 20% off a watch selling for $28 equals how large a discount? _____

6. _____% of 70 is 42.

7. 13% of 35 is _____.

8. 5 is what percent of 20? _____

9. 6 is 15 percent of what number? _____

10. If a bus with a capacity of 80 occupants is 85% full, how many more seats are available on the bus?

Worksheet 1

Find the solutions to the following problems.

1. What percent of a dollar is one nickel?

2. What is the decimal equivalent of 5 cents?

3. If n is .47, what is .47 as a percent?

4. $\frac{60}{100}$ represents what percent? What decimal?

5. N is 78% of 100. What is the value of N?

6. What is the decimal equivalent of 78%?

7. The top 35 feet of a 100-foot high flagpole is repainted. What percentage of the pole is repainted? If $\frac{35}{100}$ of the flagpole is repainted, what decimal is represented? What percent of the pole is yet to be painted? What decimal represents that percent? How many feet of the pole are yet to be painted?

8. What percent of one dollar is 100 cents? What decimal represents 100% of one dollar?

9. The Statue of Liberty is approximately 300 feet high, including the base upon which the statue stands. If the base is 150 feet high, what percent of the total height is the statue itself?

Algebra 1 Rescue! ©2004 Sopris West Educational Services. To order: 800-547-6747. Product Code 169ALG

Worksheet 2

Complete the following sentences.

> *Example:* 13% of 200 is ____.
>
> $\frac{percent}{100} = \frac{part}{whole}$
>
> $\frac{13}{100} = \frac{x}{200}$
>
> $100x = 2,600$
>
> $x = 26$

1. 35% of 28 is _____.

2. 32% of $3.00 is _____.

3. 3% of 480 is _____.

4. 40% of $25.00 is _____.

5. 75% of 900 is _____.

6. 120% of 50 is _____.

7. 50 less 20% of 50 is _____.

8. 80% of 50 is _____.

9. 40 less 20% of 50 is _____.

Write the corresponding proportions for the following problems.

> *Example:* 6 is 15% of _____.
>
> $\frac{6}{n} = \frac{15}{100}$
>
> $15n = 600$
>
> $n = 40$

10. a% of b = n.

11. 15 is 20% of n.

12. 21 is 6% of n.

13. $4.50 is 75% of $n.

14. $75 is 300% of $n.

15. m is p% of n.

Answer the following questions.

> *Example:* What % of 20 is 15?
>
> $\frac{x}{100} = \frac{15}{20}$
>
> $20x = 1,500$
>
> $x = 75$

16. What percent of 36 is 9?

17. What percent of $45 is $7.50?

18. What percent of 250 is 50?

19. What percent of 50 is 250?

20. How would you write "n% of y is z" as a proportion?

Algebra 1 Rescue! ©2004 Sopris West Educational Services. To order: 800-547-6747. Product Code 169ALG

Worksheet 3

Solve the following problems.

Example: 35% of 246 is _____. $\frac{35}{100} = \frac{x}{246}$ *or* $.35 \times 246 = x$ $x = 86.1$

1. 25% of 80 is what number?

2. 72% of 5 is what number?

3. 35% of 28 is _____.

4. 115% of 130 is _____.

Example: 90% of _____ is 72. $\frac{90}{100} = \frac{72}{x}$ $90x = 7,200$ $x = 80$

5. 3% of what number is 18.6?

6. 125% of what number is 45?

7. 1% of what number is 8.1?

8. 90% of what number is 48.6?

Example: What % of 96 is 72? $\frac{x}{100} = \frac{72}{96}$ $96x = 7,200$ $x = 75\%$ *or* $y = \frac{72}{96}$ $y = .75 = 75\%$

9. What percent of 7.5 is 45?

10. What percent of 150 is 6?

11. _____% of 70 is 28.

12. _____% of 70 is 42.

13. Before the senior class can take a field trip, 36 persons must sign up. At this time 30 have signed up. What percentage of the senior class's goal has been achieved?

14. How much will Eduardo save if the shirt he wants to buy for $21.50 is 12% off?

15. The girls' basketball team has won eight games. This is 40% of the games they have played. How many games has the team played?

16. How much sulfur is in 50 pounds of a 27% sulfur mixture?

Algebra 1 Rescue! ©2004 Sopris West Educational Services. To order: 800-547-6747. Product Code 169ALG

Posttest

1. 15% of 40 is _____.

2. 40% of _____ is 12.

3. _____% of 2,000 is 100.

4. 24 is 60% of _____.

5. 30% off a bike selling for $420 equals how large a discount? _____

6. _____% of 150 is 15.

7. 13% of 35 is _____.

8. 9 is what percent of 45? _____

9. 18 is 25% of what number? _____

10. A store is advertising 30% off all items. How much is the sale price for a CD player originally costing $60?

Chapter 3 Test—Solving Linear Equations

Objective 3-1

Solve the following equations:

1. $x + 9 = 22$

2. $-7 + n = 3$

3. $21 - x = -10$

4. $17 = n - 9$

Objective 3-2

Solve the following equations:

5. $6x = 96$

6. $\frac{y}{7} = 40$

7. $\frac{1}{5}x = 32$

8. $30 = 8x$

Objective 3-3

Solve the following equations:

9. $5x + 9 = 44$

10. $x + 6 = 3x - 14$

11. $\frac{1}{2}x - 15 = -7$

12. $-30 = 4x + 6$

Algebra 1 Rescue! ©2004 Sopris West Educational Services. To order: 800-547-6747. Product Code 169ALG

Objective 3-4

Find the solutions to the following problems:

13. The sum of three consecutive odd integers is 39. What are the integers?

14. The perimeter of a rectangle is 48 inches. The length is 17 inches. What is the width?

Objective 3-5

Solve the following proportions:

15. $\frac{2}{x} = \frac{14}{21}$

16. $\frac{4}{5} = \frac{x}{20}$

17. $\frac{2x}{8} = \frac{3}{24}$

18. $\frac{x}{20} = \frac{3}{4}$

Objective 3-6

Find the solutions to the following problems:

19. 8% of 400 is _____.

20. _____% of 80 is 4.

21. 6 is 30% of what number?

22. 15% of _____ is 45.

Pretest

Name the letter of the point in:

1. Quadrant II. _____

2. Quadrant IV. _____

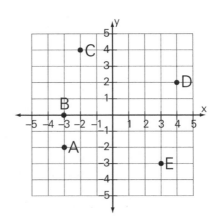

Give the ordered pairs for the letters:

3. B is ____, ____   4. A is ____, ____

5. E is ____, ____   6. C is ____, ____

Graph the following ordered pairs on the coordinate plane.

7. X (2, 5)   8. Y (−3, 1)

9. Z (0, 4)   10. N (−2, −4)

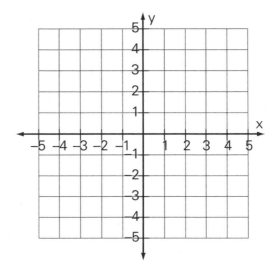

Worksheet 1

(Example) A (0, 0)   B (4, 0)   C (−4, −4)

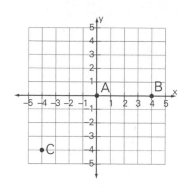

1. Name the ordered pairs for the labeled points.

    A: (_____, _____)

    B: (_____, _____)

    C: (_____, _____)

    D: (_____, _____)

    E: (_____, _____)

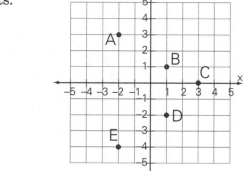

2. Plot the points listed below and label each point with its letter.

    A is (2, −3)

    B is (5, 0)

    C is (−3, −2)

    D is (−3, 4)

    E is (0, −1)

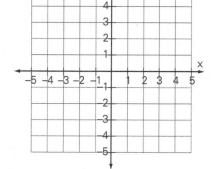

3. In the graph at the right,

    a. Name a point in Quadrant I. _____
        What is its coordinate? (_____, _____)

    b. Name a point in Quadrant IV. _____
        What is its coordinate? (_____, _____)

    c. Name a point in Quadrant II. _____
        What is its coordinate? (_____, _____)

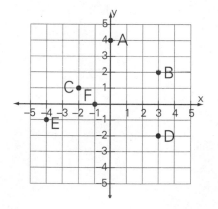

Worksheet 2

Plot the four ordered pairs on the graphs below them. Name the quadrilateral formed by connecting the four points. You may need to look up the definitions of quadrilateral, parallelogram, rectangle, trapezoid, and square.

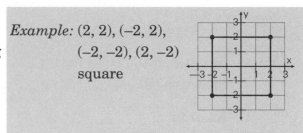

Example: (2, 2), (−2, 2), (−2, −2), (2, −2)
square

1. (2, 3), (2, −1), (−3, 1), (−3, −3)

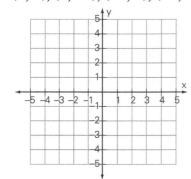

Name the quadrilateral:_____

2. (−3, −1), (−4, 2), (1, 2), (2, −1)

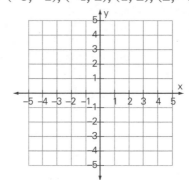

Name the quadrilateral:_____

3. (3, −1), (0, −4), (−3, −1), (0, 2)

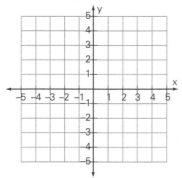

Name the quadrilateral:_____

4. (0, 2), (2, −2), (−3, −2), (−2, 2)

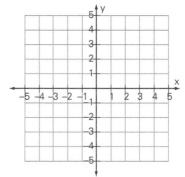

Name the quadrilateral:_____

5. (2, 0), (0, −2), (−3, 1), (−1, 3)

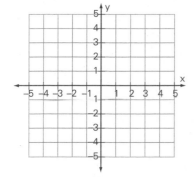

Name the quadrilateral:_____

6. (−3, −1), (2, −1), (0, −4), (−4, −4)

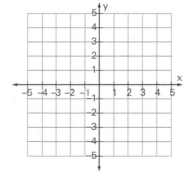

Name the quadrilateral:_____

Algebra 1 Rescue! ©2004 Sopris West Educational Services. To order: 800-547-6747. Product Code 169ALG

Posttest

Name the letter of the point in:

1. Quadrant III. _____

2. Quadrant I. _____

3. Quadrant IV. _____

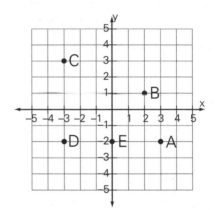

Give the ordered pairs for the letters:

4. B is ____, ____   5. D is ____, ____

6. E is ____, ____

Graph the following ordered pairs on the coordinate plane.

7. X (–5, –2)   8. Y (–3, 2)

9. Z (3, 0)   10. N (–5, 0)

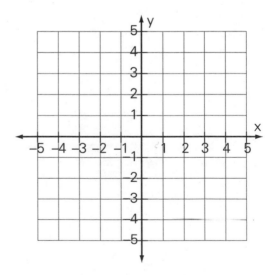

Algebra 1 Rescue! ©2004 Sopris West Educational Services. To order: 800-547-6747. Product Code 169ALG

Pretest

1. Represent the table as a set of ordered pairs called a relation.

x	y
5	2
−3	1
2	−3
−1	0
−4	−3

2. The domain of the relation in #1 is which of the following?

   a. {5, 2, 1, 0}   b. {5, −3, 2, −1, −4}

   c. {2, 1, −3, 0, −3}   d. {2, −3, −1, 0}

3. The range of the relation {(3, −1), (6, 2), (−2, −2), (0, 1)} is which of the following?

   a. {3, 6, −2, 0}   b. {−1, 2, −2, 1}

   c. {3, −1, 6, 2}   d. {−1, ...1}

4. The inverse of the relation {(−3, 4), (0, 7), (2, 9), (−1, 6)} is:

For the relation {(2, 5), (0, 8), (−1, 3)}:

5. Write the inverse relation.

6. Write the domain of the inverse relation.

7. Write the range of the inverse relation.

True or False? For the relation {(−4, 2), (6, −8), (2, 0)}:

8. The range is {−4, 6, 0}. _____

9. The domain is {−4, 6, 2}. _____

10. The inverse is {(2, 0), (6, −8), (−4, 2)}. _____

Worksheet 1

A video store charges $5.00 to rent a video for a weekend. The store gives a $5.00 discount if four or more videos are rented.

1. Make a table that shows this relation between the number of videos and the total cost for up to eight videos.

Number of Videos	Cost
1	
2	
3	
4	
5	
6	
7	
8	

2. List the ordered pairs so that the number of videos is the domain.

3. Give the range of this relation.

4. What is the inverse of this relation?

5. Graph the ordered pairs with the number of videos as the x-axis.

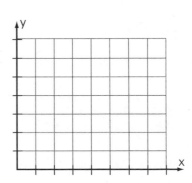

6. Write three questions that you could ask a classmate about information obtained from this relation.

Worksheet 2

The table below shows dollars earned for 1 to 5 hours of work:

Hours	Dollars Earned
1	$5.25
2	$10.50
3	$15.75
4	$21.00
5	$26.25

1. The domain is represented by what? _____

   Give the domain:_____

2. Give the range:_____

3. What would the inverse relation be?

4. Write a math question that uses this relationship between the domain and the range.

5. Describe what you would have to do to figure out how much a person would earn if he or she worked $4\frac{1}{2}$ hours.

6. Graph the relation.

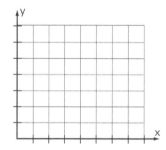

7. List the domain and range of the following relation: {(1, $4), (2, $7), (3, $10), (4, $13)}

8. Write the inverse of the relation in problem 6.

9. Write a math problem that uses this relationship between the domain and the range.

Algebra 1 Rescue! ©2004 Sopris West Educational Services. To order: 800-547-6747. Product Code 169ALG

Posttest

1. Represent the table as a set of ordered pairs called a relation.

x	y
2	5
1	−3
−3	2
0	−1
−3	−4

2. The domain of the relation in #1 is which of the following?

   a. {5, 2, 1, 0}   b. {5, −3, 2, −1, −4}

   c. {2, 1, −3, 0, −3}   d. {2, −3, −1, 0}

3. The range of the relation {(1, 0), (−2, −2), (2, 6), (−1, 3)} is which of the following?

   a. {1, 0, −2, 2, 6}   b. {0, −2, 6, 3}

   c. {1, −2, 2, −1}   d. {2, 6, −1, 3}

4. The inverse of the relation in #1 is:

The domain of the relation is {−3, 2, 0}. The range is {0, 2, −3}.

5. Write the relation in a table.

6. Write the relation as ordered pairs.

7. Write the inverse of the relation.

True or False? For the relation {(6, −4), (3, 2), (−5, 0)}:

8. The domain is {6, 3, −5.} _____

9. The range is {−4, 2, 0}. _____

10. The inverse is {(6, 0), (3, 2), (−5, −4)}. _____

Algebra 1 Rescue! ©2004 Sopris West Educational Services. To order: 800-547-6747. Product Code 169ALG

Pretest

For the equation x + y = 7 when the domain is {3, –4, 0, 1}:

1. Complete the table of values. Find the solutions of the equation x + y = 7 when the domain is {3, –4, 0, 1}.

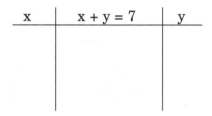

x	x + y = 7	y

2. If the domain is {0, –2, 3, –5}, find the range that would represent the solutions to the equation y = 2x –1.

3. Complete the table for any three values for x:

x	2x + y = 2	y

4. Write the ordered pairs that satisfy the equation 2x + y = 2 in #3 above.

Complete the ordered pairs to satisfy the relation y = 5 – 2x.

5. (1, _____)   6. (2, _____)   7. (–2, _____)

Complete the table to satisfy the relation 2x + y = 5.

	x	2x + y = 5	y
8.	0		
9.	–1		
10.	2		

Algebra 1 Rescue! ©2004 Sopris West Educational Services. To order: 800-547-6747. Product Code 169ALG

Worksheet 1

Example: $y = \frac{1}{2}x + 2$

If $x = -8$, then $y = \frac{1}{2}(-8) + 2$

$\qquad\qquad y = -4 + 2$

$\qquad\qquad y = -2$

Find the values for y if $y = \frac{1}{2}x + 2$.

1. a. If x = 2, then y = _____.

    b. If x = 0, then y = _____.

    c. If x = 6, then y = _____.

    d. If x = –2, then y = _____.

    e. The value we use for x is called the domain. The domain for this equation is

    _____.

2. Complete the table below for the equation y = 2x – 4. The domain is {–2, 0, 2, 4, 6}.

	x	y = 2x – 4	y	(x, y)
(Example)	–2	y = 2(–2) – 4	–8	(–2, –8)
	0			
	2			
	4			
	6			

3. Find the values for y for the equation x + y = 8. The domain is { –2, –1, 0, 2, 4}.

	x	x + y = 8	y	(x, y)
(Example)	0	0 + y = 8	8	(0, 8)
	–2			
	–1			
	2			
	4			

Algebra 1 Rescue! ©2004 Sopris West Educational Services. To order: 800-547-6747. Product Code 169ALG

Worksheet 2

1. If the domain is {–5, –3, 0, 3, 5} for the relation y = 5 – x, find the ordered pairs that satisfy the relation.

   {(_____, _____), (_____, _____), (_____, _____),

   (_____, _____), (_____, _____)}

2. Complete the table below for the domain of {–2, –1, 0, 1, 2}.

x	2x – y = 4	y	(x, y)
–2			
–1			
0			
1			
2			

3. a. Find five ordered pairs that satisfy the relation y = 2x + 1.

   {(_____, _____), (_____, _____), (_____, _____),

   (_____, _____), (_____, _____)}

   b. What is the domain?_____

   c. What is the range?_____

4. Find the ordered pairs below that satisfy the relation y – x = 4. Use the domain of {–3, –1, 0, 2, 4}.

   {(–3, _____), (–1, _____), (0, _____), (2, _____), (4, _____)}

Algebra 1 Rescue! ©2004 Sopris West Educational Services. To order: 800-547-6747. Product Code 169ALG

Worksheet 3

Match the equation with the group of ordered pairs that represent solutions to the equation. The ordered pairs are in (x, y) form. Not all sets of ordered pairs will be used.

1. $x + y = 9$

    A. {(1, 0), (0, 1), (0, 0)}

    B. {(4, 5), (3, 0), (5, 4)}

2. $y = 2x - 3$

    C. {(5, 0), (5, 4), (5, –5)}

    D. {(1, 0), (0, 1), (–1, 2)}

3. $x - y = 2$

    E. {(0, 5), (4, 5), (–5, 5)}

    F. {(3, 3), (1, 1), (–1, –1)}

4. $y = -x$

    G. {(4, 5), (–1, –5), (1, –1)}

5. $2x + y = 5$

    H. {(5, 3), (0, –2), (3, 1)}

    I. {(1, 0), (2, 3), (0, –3)}

6. $2x + 2y = 2$

    J. {(2, 3), (0, 4), (4, 2)}

    K. {(2, 1), (–3, 11), (4, –3)}

7. $6x - 2y = 6$

    L. {(3, –3), (–3, 3), (–3, 0)}

    M. {(0, 0), (–2, 4), (1, –2)}

8. $y = -2x$

    N. {(2, 1), (–3, –1), (4, 3)}

9. $x = 5$

    O. {(4, 5), (8, 1), (2, 7)}

    P. {(3, –3), (4, –4), (0, 0)}

10. $x + 2y = 8$

    Q. {(0, 0), (4, –2), (1, –2)}

Algebra 1 Rescue! ©2004 Sopris West Educational Services. To order: 800-547-6747. Product Code 169ALG

Posttest

1. Complete the table for the following domain: {0, 1, –3, 2}

x	y = x – 3	y

2. Find the solutions of the linear equation y = 2x + 2 when the domain is {0, –1, 2, –2}.

3. The linear equation 2x + 2y = 6 has a domain of {1, 2, 3, 4}. What is the range?

4. Complete the table for any three values for x:

x	y = 2 – 2x	y

5. Write the ordered pairs that satisfy the equation y = 2 – 2x in #4 above.

Complete the ordered pairs to satisfy the relation y = 3x + 1.

6. (0, _____) 7. (–3, _____) 8. (3, _____)

Complete the table to satisfy the relation 3x + y = 5.

	x	3x + y = 5	y	(x, y)
9.	–1			
10.	2			

Algebra 1 Rescue! ©2004 Sopris West Educational Services. To order: 800-547-6747. Product Code 169ALG

Pretest

Complete the table and construct the graph for problems 1–6.

1. y – 3x = 4

x	y – 3x = 4	y	(x, y)
–2			
–1			
0			
1			

2. Graph of y – 3x = 4

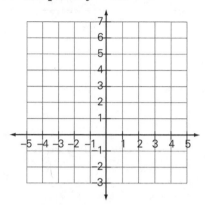

3. 4x + 2y = 6

x	4x + 2y = 6	y	(x, y)
–1			
0			
2			
3			

4. Graph of 4x + 2y = 6

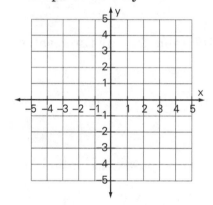

5. y = x

x	y = x	y	(x, y)
3			
0			
–2			

6. Graph of y = x

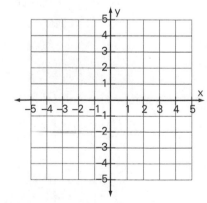

Algebra 1 Rescue! ©2004 Sopris West Educational Services. To order: 800-547-6747. Product Code 169ALG

Pretest (continued)

Make a table and construct the graph for problems 7–10.

7. x + y = 2

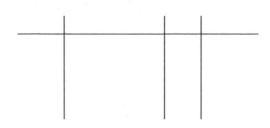

8. Graph of x + y = 2

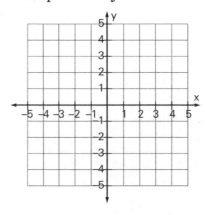

9. y + 2x = 0

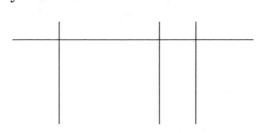

10. Graph of y + 2x = 0

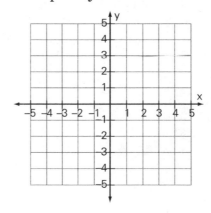

Worksheet 1

Find three ordered pairs for each equation and graph them.

Example:	$y - 2x = 4$
	$y = 4 + 2x$
	$(2, 8), (0, 4), (-1, 2)$

1. $y = 2x - 1$

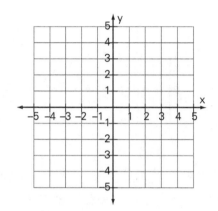

2. $y = 2 - x$

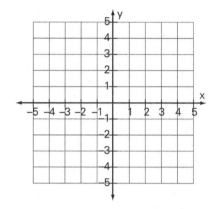

3. $y = x$

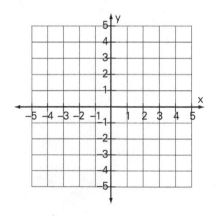

4. $2x + y = 3$

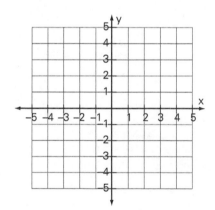

Algebra 1 Rescue! ©2004 Sopris West Educational Services. To order: 800-547-6747. Product Code 169ALG

Worksheet 1 (continued)

5. y = 4

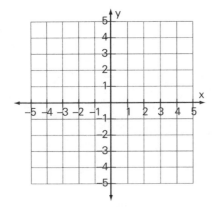

6. y = 4x

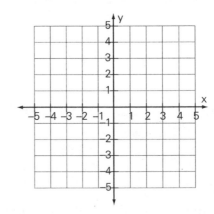

7. y − 5x = 2

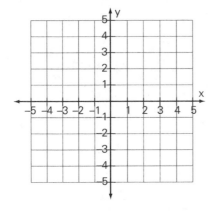

8. 2x + 2y = 8

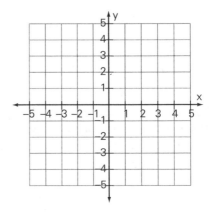

Worksheet 2

1. Find the ordered pair solutions for $y = 2x - 1$ when the domain is {1, 2, 3, 4}. Graph these ordered pairs.

   {(_____, _____), (_____, _____),
   (_____, _____), (_____, _____)}

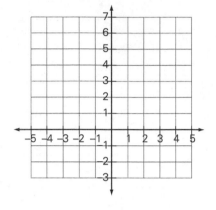

2. Complete the table and graph the equation $x - y = 4$.

x	x – y = 4	y	(x, y)
1			
0			
–2			
2			

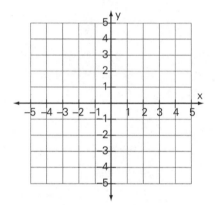

3. Choose any three values of x and find the range for the linear equation $2x + y = -3$. Graph these ordered pairs and the equation $2x + y = -3$.

   {(_____, _____), (_____, _____),
   (_____, _____)}

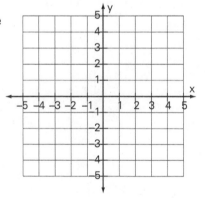

Algebra 1 Rescue! ©2004 Sopris West Educational Services. To order: 800-547-6747. Product Code 169ALG

Worksheet 2 (continued)

4. If the domain is {−1, 0, 1, 2}, graph the relation
   y = −2x + 4.

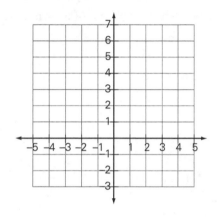

5. Complete the table and graph the equation x + y = −2.

x	x + y = −2	y	(x, y)
0	0 + y = −2		
	x + 2 = −2	2	
−1			
		0	

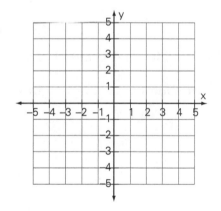

Worksheet 3

Tell whether each equation is a linear equation and tell why or why not.

1. $3x + 7y = 10$

2. $\frac{1}{2}x = y + 5$

3. $y = x^2$

4. $y = x^2 + 4$

5. $x^2 + 2x = y$

6. $xy = 12$

Tell whether the graph of each equation will be a straight line. Graph any that you are not sure of.

7. $y = 2x + 1$	8. $2x = 3y$	9. $x + 4 = 0$
10. $4x + 3y = 6$	11. $y = x^2$	12. $y = x^2 + 2x$

All equations that graph a straight line are called _____ equations.

Put the following equations in linear form and also in the form when y is solved in terms of x.

13. $2x + y = 4$	14. $3x = 5y$
15. $2x - 8 = -y$	16. $\frac{1}{3}y = 2x$
17. $2x - y = 7$	18. $\frac{2}{3}y = 12x$

Graph the equations in problems 8, 13, and 15:

8. $2x = 3y$	13. $2x + y = 4$	15. $2x - 8 = -y$

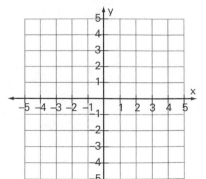 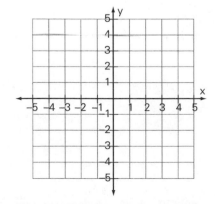 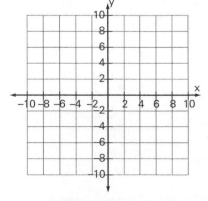

Algebra 1 Rescue! ©2004 Sopris West Educational Services. To order: 800-547-6747. Product Code 169ALG

Posttest

Complete the tables and construct the graphs for problems 1–6.

1. $y - 2x = 3$

x	y − 2x = 3	y	(x, y)
−2			
−1			
0			
2			

2. Graph of $y - 2x = 3$

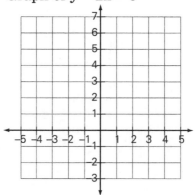

3. $2x + 3y = 10$

x	2x + 3y = 10	y	(x, y)
5			
2			
−1			
−4			

4. Graph of $2x + 3y = 10$

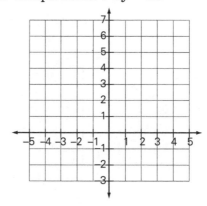

5. $y = 2x$

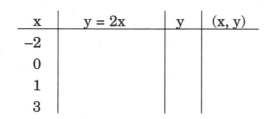

x	y = 2x	y	(x, y)
−2			
0			
1			
3			

6. Graph of $y = 2x$

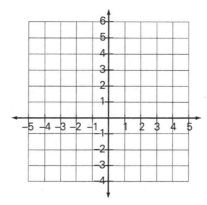

Posttest (continued)

Make a table of values and construct the graphs for problems 7–10.

7. x + 2y = –6

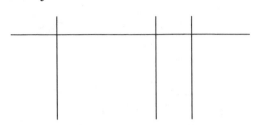

8. Graph of x + 2y = –6

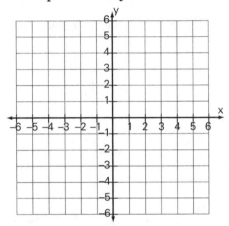

9. x + y = 15

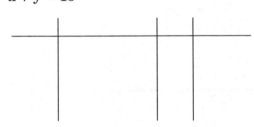

10. Graph of x + y = 15

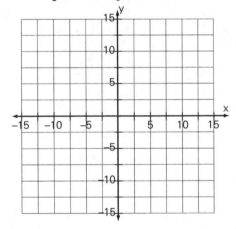

Algebra 1 Rescue! ©2004 Sopris West Educational Services. To order: 800-547-6747. Product Code 169ALG

Pretest

Determine whether each of the following is a function:

1. $\{(2, 3), (4, 5), (-1, 6), (-4, 5)\}$

2. $\{(-2, 0), (1, 2), (3, -2), (4, -1), (0, -3)\}$

3.

x	y
2	3
-3	0
5	8
-1	2

4.

x	y
-7	5
3	2
7	-1
3	6
4	-3

Find the value of the function $f(x) = 3x - 3$ for:

5. $f(2)$

6. $f(-1)$

Find the value of the function $f(x) = x^2 + 2$ for:

7. $f(-2)$

8. $f(3)$

Find the value of the function $f(x) = x^2 - 2x + 1$ for:

9. $f(1)$

10. $f(-2)$

Worksheet 1

1. Determine whether the relation shown is a function:

   a. {(2, –3), (3, 6), (5, –8), (1, 2)}

   b. {(1, 5), (1, –2), (1, 0), (1, 3)}

   c. {(1, 4), (–2, 4), (3, 4), (0, 4)}

2. Determine whether the relation shown is a function:

   a.
x	y
–3	3
–2	4
2	4
0	2
4	4

   b.
x	y
–4	3
3	2
–4	1
–3	0
–4	0

3. Determine whether the relation shown is a function:

   a.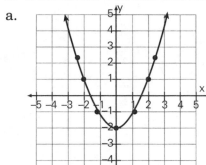

   b.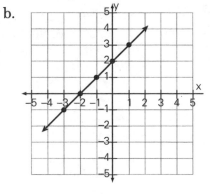

   c.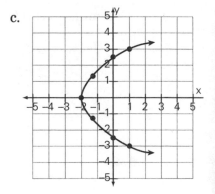

   d.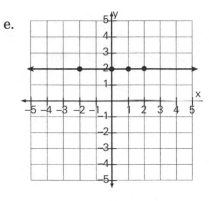

   e.

Worksheet 2

Example: If f(x) = 5x + 0, find each value for f(6), f(–3).
$$f(6) = 5(6) + 0 = 30$$
$$f(–3) = 5(–3) + 0 = –15$$

1. If f(x) = 3x – 2, find each value:

    a. f(6) = _____

    b. f(–2) = _____

    c. f(2) = _____

2. If f(x) = x² – 1, find each value:

    a. f(3) = _____

    b. f(–3) = _____

    c. f(0) = _____

3. If f(x) = 3x + 2, find each value:

    a. f(–4) = _____

    b. f(–2) = _____

    c. f(w) = _____

4. If f(x) = x² – 2x, find each value:

    a. f(–4) = _____

    b. f(4) = _____

    c. f(1.5) = _____

5. Find three values given for each relation and determine if it is a function.

    a. $f(x) = \sqrt{x}$

    b. $f(x) = \pm|x|$

Posttest

1. Determine which is the value of f(4) for the function f(x) = 2x + 2.

   a. 8   b. 4   c. 10   d. 6

Find the value of the function $f(x) = 8 - x^2$ for:

2. f(3)   3. f(−1)

Determine which of the following is a function:

4. {(−2, 1), (3, 0), (−2, 4), (0, −5), (1, 2)}

5. {(6, 3), (5, −2), (2, 4), (−1, −1)}

6.

x	y
−1	4
5	2
3	−6
0	1

7.

x	y
2	4
6	8
8	4
10	8
2	8

8. Determine which is the value of f(−1) for the function f(x) = 6 − 3x.

   a. 9   b. 3   c. −3   d. 6

Find the value of the function $f(x) = 4 - 2x^2$ for:

9. f(2)   10. f(−2)

Algebra 1 Rescue! ©2004 Sopris West Educational Services. To order: 800-547-6747. Product Code 169ALG

Chapter 4 Test—Graphing Relations and Functions

Objective 4-1

Use the graphs to complete problems 1–4.

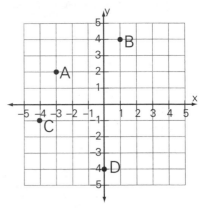

1. Name the ordered pair for letter A. (_____ , _____)

2. Name a point in Quadrant III. _____

3. Graph the ordered pair P (–1, 2).

4. Graph the ordered pair Q (3, 1).

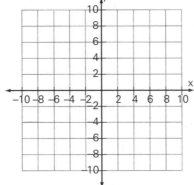

Objective 4-2

Given the relation {(2, 1), (–1, 3), (5, 8), (0, 6)}, answer problems 5–8.

5. The range of the relation is _____.

6. The inverse of the relation is _____.

7. The domain of the relation is _____.

8. The domain of the inverse relation is _____.

Objective 4-3

Find the range values given the domain and relation.

9. $y = x - 3$

x	y
-2	
0	
3	
8	

10. $x + y = 7$

x	x + y = 7	y
-4		
-2		
0		
2		
4		

11. $2x - 2y = 3$

x	2x - 2y = 8	y
-2		
0		
4		
8		

12. Find the ordered pairs that satisfy the relation $y = 6 - x$ when the domain is {3, 6, 0, -5}.

Objective 4-4

Make a table of values for each relation and construct the graph.

13. $x - y = 7$

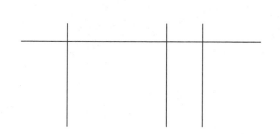

14. Graph of $x - y = 7$

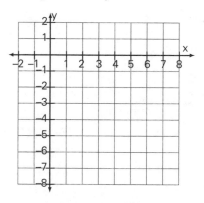

15. $2x = y - 3$

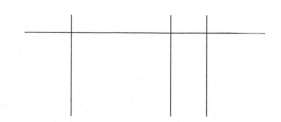

16. Graph of $2x = y - 3$

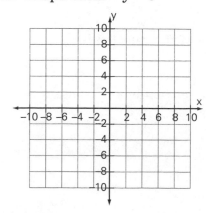

Objective 4-5

Determine if each of the following (problems 17–19) are functions.

17. {(2, 3), (3, 4), (6, 7), (7, 6)}

18. {(2, 8), (–2, 5), (0, 7), (–2, –5)}

19.

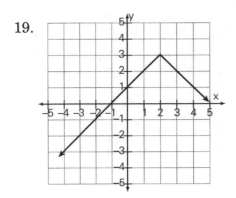

20. Given f(x) = 4x – 12, find f(–4).

Pretest

1. Find the slope.

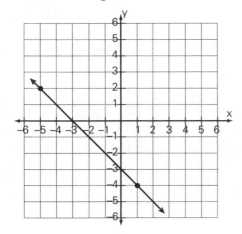

2. Find the slope.

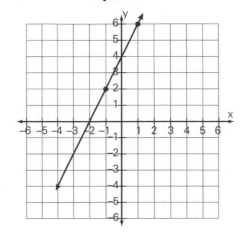

3. Find the slope of the line that contains the points $(2, 0)$, $(3, 2)$.

4. Find the slope of the line that contains the points $(-3, 5)$, $(-1, 6)$.

5. Find the slope of the line that contains the points $(5, 0)$, $(0, 10)$.

Worksheet 1

Name the slope for each graph.

1.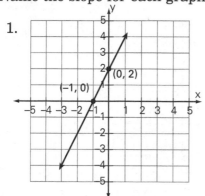

2.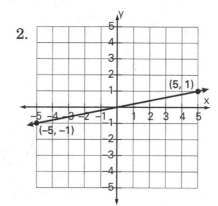

3.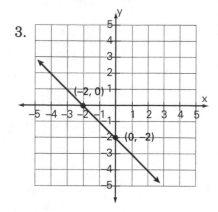

4.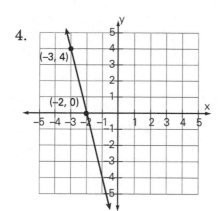

5.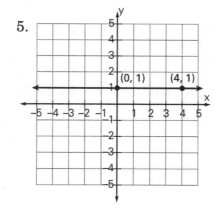

6.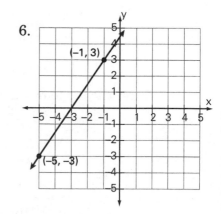

7.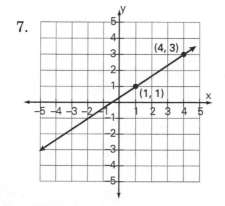

8.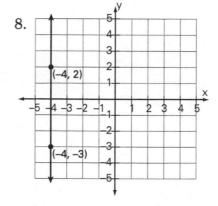

9.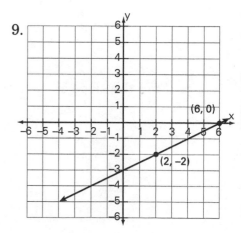

Algebra 1 Rescue! ©2004 Sopris West Educational Services. To order: 800-547-6747. Product Code 169ALG

Worksheet 2

Find the slope of each line.

1.

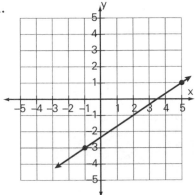

2.

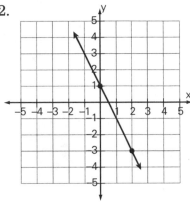

3.

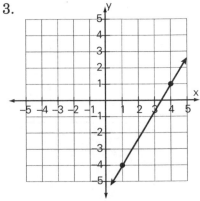

Find the slope using $m = \frac{(y_2 - y_1)}{(x_2 - x_1)}$.

4. $(2, 6), (-2, 4)$

5. $(-7, -2), (3, 3)$

6. $(1, 8), (4, -4)$

Find the slope.

7.

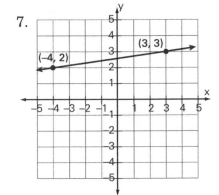

8.

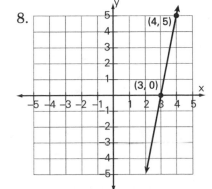

9.

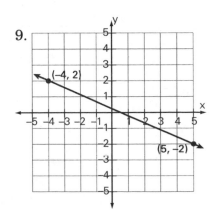

Worksheet 3

1. Draw the graph of $y + 3 = x$.
   What is the slope?

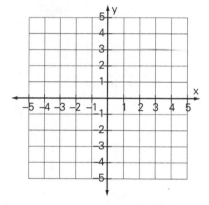

2. Draw the graph of $2x + y = 0$.
   What is the slope?

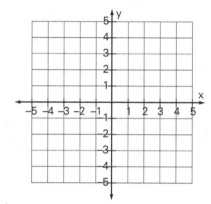

3. Draw the graph of $2y = 2x + 8$.
   What is the slope?

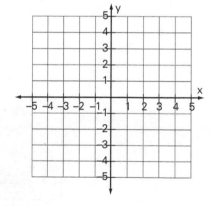

4. What is the slope of a line that contains $(2, 5)$ and $(3, 1)$? Sketch the graph.

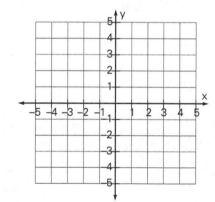

Algebra 1 Rescue! ©2004 Sopris West Educational Services. To order: 800-547-6747. Product Code 169ALG

Posttest

1. Find the slope.

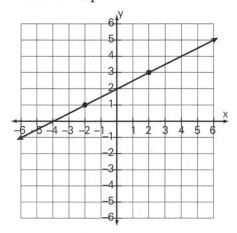

2. Find the slope.

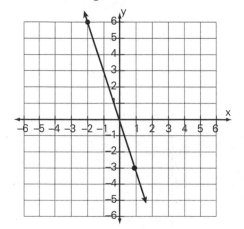

3. Find the slope of the line that contains the points (3, 4), (2, 7).

4. Find the slope of the line that contains the points (10, 6), (2, 2).

5. Find the slope of the line that contains the points (–3, 4), (5, 6).

Pretest

Find the equation of each line from the given information. Write the equation in standard form. Show your steps.

1.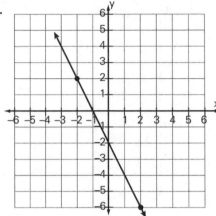

2.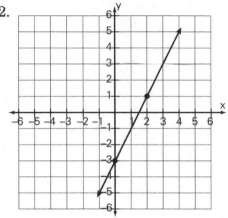

3. Contains points (−1, 5), (1, −3).

4. Slope of 2 and contains (1, 1).

5. Contains points (1, 6), (3, 2).

Worksheet 1

Example:

a. Find the slope m.

$$m = \frac{(y_2 - y_1)}{(x_2 - x_1)} = \frac{[0 - (-2)]}{(3 - 0)} = \frac{+2}{3}$$

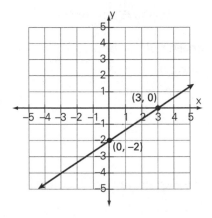

b. Find the equation of the line using the slope
   and the point (0, –2).

$$m = \frac{(y_2 - y_1)}{(x_2 - x_1)} \text{ or } m = \frac{y - (-2)}{x - 0}$$

$$\frac{2}{3} = \frac{y + 2}{x}$$

$$2x = 3y + 6$$

c. Write the above equation in standard form ax + by = c. (2x – 3y = 6) Find the equation of
   the line using the point-slope form and the point (0, –2).

$$y - y_1 = m(x - x_1)$$

Note: $\frac{m}{1} = \frac{(y_2 - y_1)}{(x_2 - x_1)} = m(x - x_1) = (y - y_1) \text{ or } y - y_1 = m(x - x_1)$

$$y - (-2) = \frac{2}{3}(x - 0)$$

$$y + 2 = \frac{2}{3}x \text{ (point-slope form)}$$

---

1. a. Find the slope of the line.

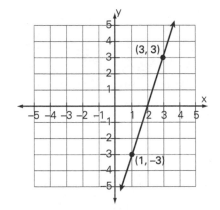

   b. Write the point-slope equation of the line.

   $$y - y_1 = m(x - x_1)$$

   c. Write the equation in standard form.

   $$ax + by = c$$

Algebra 1 Rescue! ©2004 Sopris West Educational Services. To order: 800-547-6747. Product Code 169ALG

Worksheet 1 (continued)

2. a. Given the slope of a line is –2 and it contains the point (4, 1), write the point-slope equation.

   $y - y_1 = m(x - x_1)$

   b. Write the equation in standard form ax + by = c.

3. Find the equation of a line containing the points (–2, –4), (1, 5). Use the following steps.

   a. Find the slope. $m = \frac{(y_2 - y_1)}{(x_2 - x_1)}$

   b. Write the equation in point-slope form. $y - y_1 = m(x - x_1)$

   c. Write the equation in standard form. ax + by = c

4. Find the equation of a line containing the points (3, –1), (2, 2). Write the equation in the point-slope form and the standard form.

5. Find the equation of a line with slope 1 and containing the point (–1, –1). Write the equation in the point-slope form and the standard form.

Algebra 1 Rescue! ©2004 Sopris West Educational Services. To order: 800-547-6747. Product Code 169ALG

Worksheet 2

Write the equation in the point-slope form $(y - y_1) = m(x - x_1)$ for the line containing the point and slope given.

1. (3, 4), slope of –1

2. (–3, 1), slope of 2

3. (0, 0), slope of 6

4. (3, 3), slope of $\frac{1}{2}$

5. (–5, –1), slope of –4

6. (6, –3), slope of $-1\frac{1}{2}$

The following equations are written in point-slope form. Rewrite them in standard form (ax + by = c).

7. $(y - 3) = 2(x + 2)$

8. $(y + 2) = -1(x - 5)$

9. $y - 6 = -3(x + 3)$

10. $y + 2 = -\frac{1}{2}(x + 6)$

Write the equation in standard form for the line containing the point and slope given.

11. (2, 4), m = 4

12. (–1, 4), m = –2

13. (–2, –4), m = $\frac{1}{4}$

14. ($\frac{1}{2}$, 3), m = 8

Algebra 1 Rescue! ©2004 Sopris West Educational Services. To order: 800-547-6747. Product Code 169ALG

Worksheet 3

Find the equation of each line given in the graphs below. Write the equation in standard form.

1.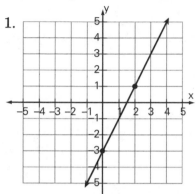

2.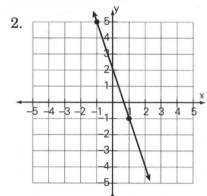

Find the equation of a line containing the two points. Write the equation in standard form.

3. (4, 1), (3, 3)

4. (−1, 2), (−4, −4)

5. (1, 7), (−4, 2)

6. (−2, 3), (2, 5)

Find the equation of a line with the point and slope given below. Write the equation in standard form.

7. (4, 6), m = $\frac{1}{2}$

8. (−1, −5), m = −2

Algebra 1 Rescue! ©2004 Sopris West Educational Services. To order: 800-547-6747. Product Code 169ALG

Posttest

Find the equation of each line from the given information. Write the equation in standard form. Show your steps.

1.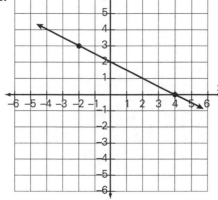

2.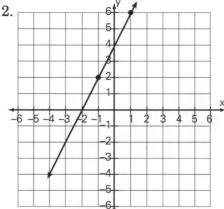

3. Contains points $(1, 5)$, $(-3, 3)$.

4. Slope of -1 and contains $(1, 3)$.

5. Contains points $(1, 0)$, $(3, 6)$.

Algebra 1 Rescue! ©2004 Sopris West Educational Services. To order: 800-547-6747. Product Code 169ALG

Pretest

Draw the best-fit line, if it exists, and name the equation for the best-fit line.

Note: Answers will vary. Have the students show their work.

1.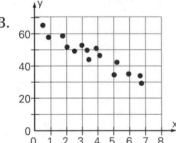

2.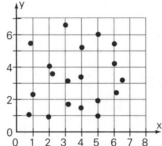

3.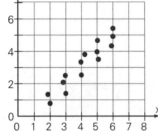

4.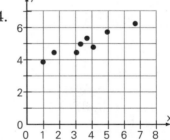

5.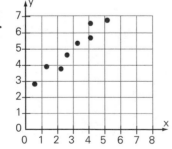

Worksheet 1

Draw the best-fit lines for the following graphs.

1.
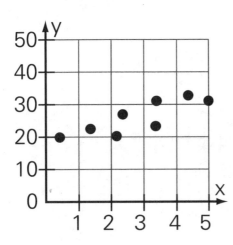

2.
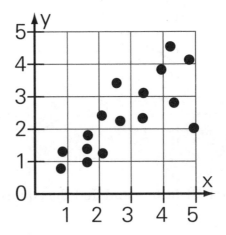

Find the equation of the best-fit line in the following graphs. (Find the slope and then the equation.)

3.
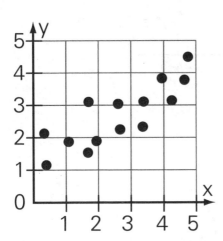

4.
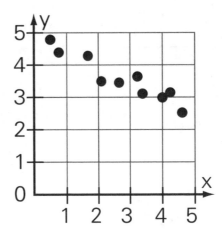

Worksheet 2

Which line—A, B, or C—is the best-fit line for the points graphed?

1.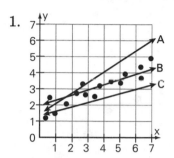

2.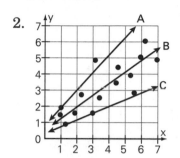

Draw the best-fit line and find the equation.

3.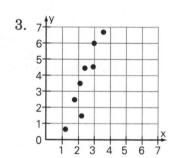

4.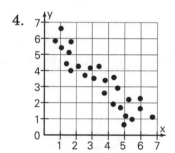

5.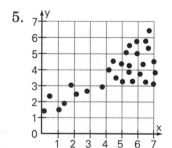

6.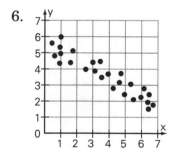

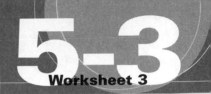

Worksheet 3

1. The information below represents the high scores earned on a video arcade game and the number of games played. Make a graph of the information.

Name	Games	High Score
Juan	8 games	2,000
Tim	2 games	600
Sally	10 games	2,500
Fran	6 games	1,400
Bill	7 games	1,700
Jordan	4 games	1,100
Andy	3 games	800

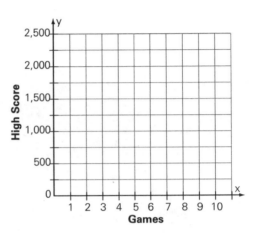

2. Draw the best-fit line for these data. What is the equation of the best-fit line? Explain what the equation represents. What would you predict for a high score if a person played 20 games?

Posttest

Draw the best-fit line, if it exists, and name the equation for the best-fit line.

Note: Answers will vary. Have the students show their work.

1.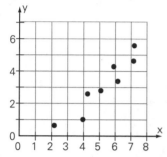

2.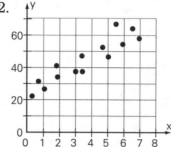

3.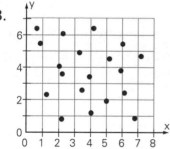

4.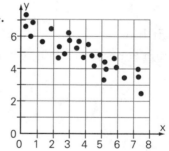

5.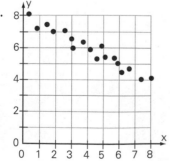

Pretest

1. a. Write the equation x + y = 1 in slope-intercept form.

    b. What is the slope?

    c. What is the y-intercept?

    d. Sketch the graph.

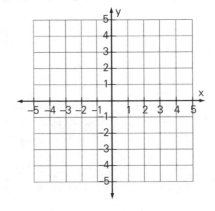

2. a. Write the equation y – 8 = 2x in slope-intercept form.

    b. What is the slope?

    c. What is the y-intercept?

    d. Sketch the graph.

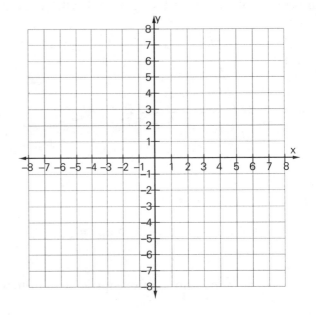

3. a. Write the equation y – 2x = 6 in slope-intercept form.

    b. What is the slope?

    c. What is the y-intercept?

Worksheet 1

Definition: The y-intercept is the y value where the graph intersects the y-axis. The x-intercept is the x value where the graph intersects the x-axis.

Example: $y = -\frac{1}{3}x + 1$

Let $x = 0 \rightarrow y = 1$
(0, 1)

Let $y = 0 \rightarrow x = 3$
(3, 0)

x-intercept is 3
y-intercept is 1

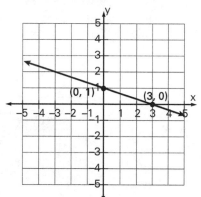

Name the y-intercept and x-intercept (when x = 0 and when y = 0) in the graphs below.

1.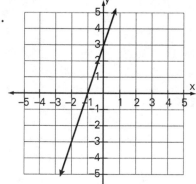

y-intercept = _____; x-intercept = _____

2.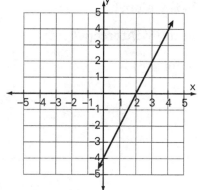

y-intercept = _____; x-intercept = _____

Find the y-intercept and x-intercept for the following equations.

3. $y = x + 6$

4. $y = -2x + 8$

5. $y = \frac{1}{2}x + 5$

6. $x + y = -2$

7. $x + 2y = 10$

8. $y - 2x = 6$

Algebra 1 Rescue! ©2004 Sopris West Educational Services. To order: 800-547-6747. Product Code 169ALG

Worksheet 2

Sketch the following graphs from the given information.

1. x-intercept is 3
   y-intercept is −2

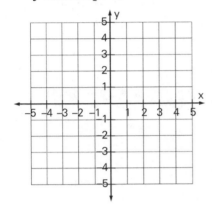

2. slope is 2
   y-intercept is 1

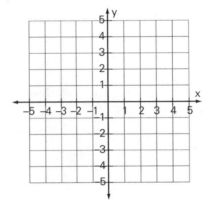

3. slope is ½
   x-intercept is −2

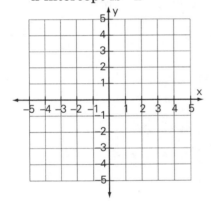

4. x-intercept is 3
   y-intercept is 3

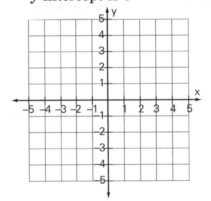

5. slope is −1
   y-intercept is 2

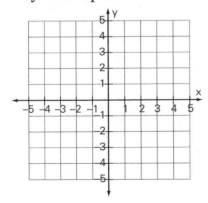

6. slope is 2
   y-intercept is 0

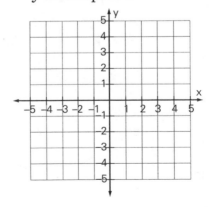

Worksheet 3

Write the following linear equations in the slope-intercept form (y = mx + b). Name the slope and y-intercept (when x = 0).

1. x + y = 6

2. y + 3 = x

3. 4x + 4y = 20

4. x − y = 7

5. x = y + 1

6. x + 2y + 3 = 0

7. 2x + 3y = 9

8. $\frac{1}{2}$y = x − 4

9. .3x + y = 5

Write the following equations in the slope-intercept form and sketch the graph.

10. 2x − y = 2

11. 2y + 4x − 6 = 0

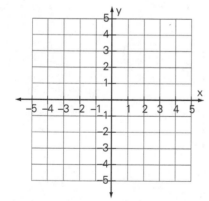

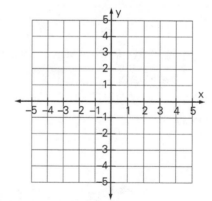

12. 3y − 3 = 6x

13. x + .5y = −1

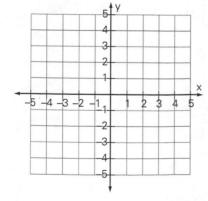

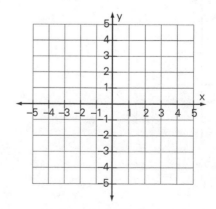

Algebra 1 Rescue! ©2004 Sopris West Educational Services. To order: 800-547-6747. Product Code 169ALG

Worksheet 4

Rewrite each of the following linear equations in the slope-intercept form. Name the slope and y-intercept and sketch the graph.

1. $x = 2y + 4$

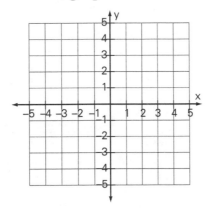

2. $x + y = 3$

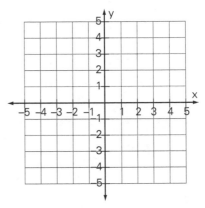

3. $4x + 4y = 20$

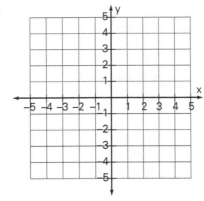

4. $4y - 2x = 4$

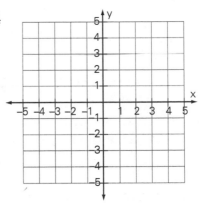

5. $x + \frac{1}{2}y + 2 = 0$

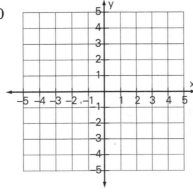

6. $5x = 5y + 10$

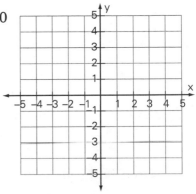

Posttest

1. a. Write the equation $2x - y + 4 = 0$ in slope-intercept form.

    b. What is the slope?

    c. What is the y-intercept?

    d. Sketch the graph.

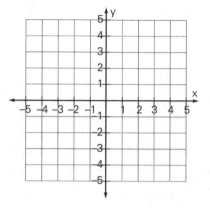

2. a. Write the equation $x = 2y - 4$ in slope-intercept form.

    b. What is the slope?

    c. What is the y-intercept?

    d. Sketch the graph.

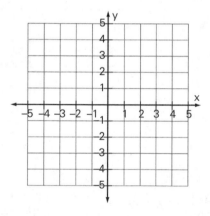

3. a. Write the equation $2x - 4 = y + 2$ in slope-intercept form.

    b. What is the slope?

    c. What is the y-intercept?

Algebra 1 Rescue! ©2004 Sopris West Educational Services. To order: 800-547-6747. Product Code 169ALG

Pretest

Indicate if the graphs of the two equations in each problem would be parallel, perpendicular, or neither.

1. $y = 2x + 3$
   $y = \frac{1}{2}x + 7$

2. $x + y = 4$
   $x - y = 2$

3. $2x + 3y = 6$
   $3 - 2x = 3y$

4. $x + y = 3x - 2$
   $2x = y + 4$

5. $x - 2y = 4$
   $x - 2y = 6$

6. $y - 1 = 3x$
   $3y - x = 6$

7. $y = 2x + 8$
   $6 - 2y = x$

8. $4x + 3y = 12$
   $3y = -4x + 9$

9. $2x + y = 12$
   $\frac{1}{2}y = 6 - x$

10. $x + y = 4$
    $6 - y = x$

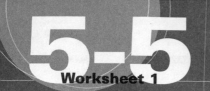

Worksheet 1

1. Write the equations for the lines on the graph that are parallel.

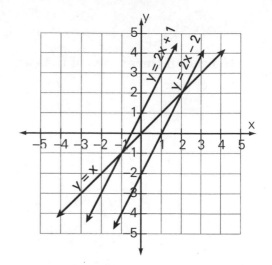

2. Can you tell by looking at the equations if the graph of the two lines will be parallel? If so, how?

In each problem below, circle the two equations whose graphs will be parallel. (Sketch the graphs if necessary.)

3. $y = x + 4$ $y = x - 10$ $y = 4 - x$

4. $y = 3x + 6$ $y = 2x - 8$ $y = 2x - 6$

5. $y = -x + 1$ $y = x + 1$ $y = -x + 3$

6. $x + y = 2$ $y = 3 - x$ $y = x + 2$

7. $2x - y = 4$ $y = 4 + x$ $y = 2x + 4$

8. $7x = y$ $y = 7x + 2$ $y = 2x - 7$

Name an equation whose graph will be parallel to the graph of the equation given.

9. $y = 2x - 1$ 10. $y = 4x + 1$ 11. $x + y = 1$

12. $y = 3 - x$ 13. $4 - y = x$ 14. $y = 9x$

Worksheet 2

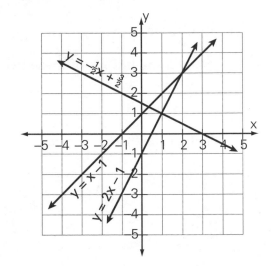

1. Write the equations for the lines on the graph that are perpendicular.

2. What relationship do you see between the slopes of lines that are perpendicular?

In each problem below, circle the two equations whose graphs will be perpendicular. (Sketch the graphs if necessary.)

3. $y = 3x + 1$ $y = x + 3$ $y = -\frac{1}{3}x + 2$

4. $y = x + 4$ $y = -x + 1$ $y = 2x - 3$

5. $y = 2x + 1$ $y = \frac{1}{2}x - 1$ $y = -\frac{1}{2}x + 2$

6. $y + 2x = 4$ $y - 2x = -4$ $y = \frac{1}{2}x + 1$

7. $3 - 2y = x$ $y = -2x + 4$ $2x - y = 5$

8. $y + x = \frac{1}{7}$ $y = 7x - 3$ $y + \frac{1}{7}x = 1$

Name an equation whose graph will be perpendicular to the graph of the equation given.

9. $y = \frac{1}{2}x + 3$ 10. $y = x + 1$

11. $y = \frac{1}{4}x - 4$ 12. $2x - y = 4$

13. $x - 2y = 8$ 14. $5y + x = 10$

Worksheet 3

1. Sketch the graphs of these two equations:

   $y = 2x - 1$

   $y = 2x + 3$

2. The graphs from #1 are _____.

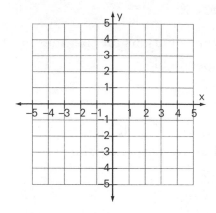

3. Sketch the graphs of these two equations:

   $y = 3x - 1$

   $y = -\frac{1}{3}x + 1$

4. The graphs from #3 are _____.

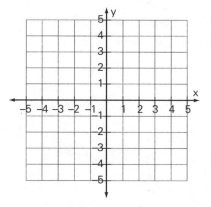

5. Tell whether each pair of equations below are parallel or perpendicular.

   a. $y = x + 1$ $y = -x + 2$

   b. $y = \frac{1}{2}x - 1$ $y = -2x + 3$

   c. $y = 5x + 4$ $y = 5x + \frac{1}{5}$

   d. $x + 2y = 4$ $2x - y = 4$

6. Sketch the graphs of the equations below.

   $y = 2x - 3$

   $9 + 3y = 6x$

7. What can be said about the graphs of the equations in #6?

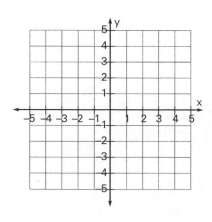

Posttest

Indicate if the graphs of the two equations in each problem would be parallel, perpendicular, or neither.

1. $y = 3x + 4$
   $y = 4x + 3$

2. $x + y = 7$
   $y - 3 = x$

3. $2x + y = 4$
   $y = \frac{1}{2}x - 1$

4. $y = 4x - 1$
   $4x - y = 4$

5. $2x - 3y = 8$
   $8 - 2x = -3y$

6. $2y + 4 = 3x$
   $2x + 3y = 3$

7. $x + y = 8$
   $y - x = 2$

8. $y + x = 2x + 3$
   $y - x = 7$

9. $2x + y = 12$
   $\frac{1}{2}y = 6 - x$

10. $x + y = 4$
    $6 - y = x$

Chapter 5 Test—Analyzing Linear Equations

Objective 5-1

1. What is the slope of the line?

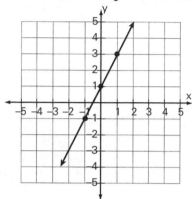

2. Find the slope of a line that contains the points (5, 6), (1, 4).

Objective 5-2

3. What is the slope of the line? What is the equation of the line in standard form?

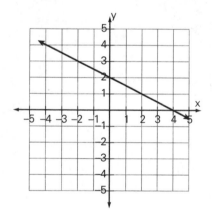

4. Write, in standard form, the equation of a line that contains the points (3, 0), (4, 6). Show your work.

Algebra 1 Rescue! ©2004 Sopris West Educational Services. To order: 800-547-6747. Product Code 169ALG

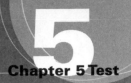
Objective 5-3

Draw the best-fit line and name the equation of the best-fit line. Write the equation in slope-intercept form.

5.

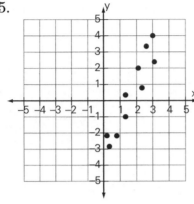

6.

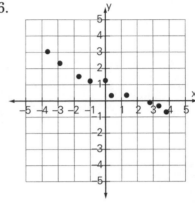

Objective 5-4

7. a. Write the equation $y - 2x = -3$ in the slope-intercept form.

    b. What is the slope?

    c. What is the y-intercept?

    d. Sketch the graph.

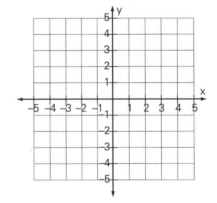

Objective 5-5

Indicate if the graphs of the two equations given in each of the following problems would be parallel or perpendicular.

8. $y = 2x + 3$ $x + 2y = -8$

9. $6x - 2y = -8$ $y + 2 = 3x$

Pretest

Solve and graph the solution set for each inequality.

1. $f + 7 < 4$

-7 -6 -5 -4 -3 -2 -1 0 1 2 3 4 5 6 7

2. $y - 3 \geq -6$

-7 -6 -5 -4 -3 -2 -1 0 1 2 3 4 5 6 7

3. $g + 8 \leq 10$

-7 -6 -5 -4 -3 -2 -1 0 1 2 3 4 5 6 7

4. $h - 3 > 2$

-7 -6 -5 -4 -3 -2 -1 0 1 2 3 4 5 6 7

5. $y + 6 \geq 10$

-7 -6 -5 -4 -3 -2 -1 0 1 2 3 4 5 6 7

6. $x - 8 < 2$

-3 -2 -1 0 1 2 3 4 5 6 7 8 9 10 11

7. $a - 5 > -8$

-7 -6 -5 -4 -3 -2 -1 0 1 2 3 4 5 6 7

8. $b + 7 \leq 3$

-7 -6 -5 -4 -3 -2 -1 0 1 2 3 4 5 6 7

9. $x - 3 > -6$

-7 -6 -5 -4 -3 -2 -1 0 1 2 3 4 5 6 7

10. $y + 7 \leq 7$

-7 -6 -5 -4 -3 -2 -1 0 1 2 3 4 5 6 7

Worksheet 1

Construct the linear graph for each inequality.

Example: x < 8

1. x > 2

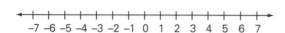

2. x ≥ −4

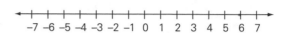

3. x < 3

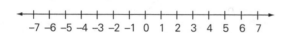

4. x ≤ −1

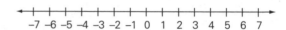

5. x < −2

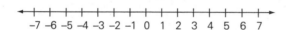

6. x < 10

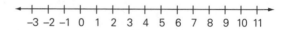

7. x > 5

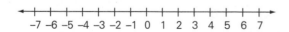

8. x ≥ −2

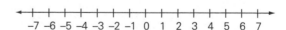

9. x > −3

10. x ≥ 4

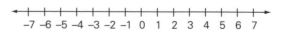

Worksheet 2

Solve each inequality and graph the solution on the number line.

Example: $x + 4 < 2$
              $(x + 4) - 4 < 2 - 4$
              $x < -2$

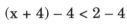

1. $x + 3 < 9$

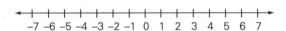

2. $w - 7 > -4$

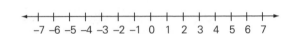

3. $a - 12 \leq 6$

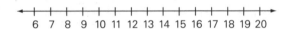

4. $y + 14 \geq 23$

5. $b + 6 \geq -2$

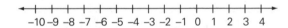

6. $h - 10 \leq 4$

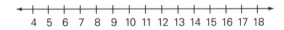

7. $5 < t - 6$

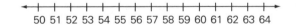

8. $-9 \geq c - 7$

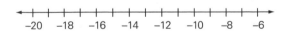

9. $x - 34 < 27$

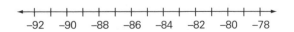

10. $y + 37 \geq 18$

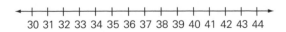

11. $64 + k > -26$

12. $d - 34 \geq 0$

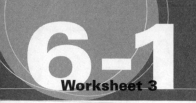
Worksheet 3

Solve each of the following, and graph the solution set on the number line.

Example: $a - 7 \geq -3$

$(a - 7) + 7 \geq -3 + 7$

$a \geq 4$

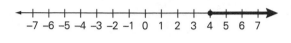

1. $x + 8 < 2$

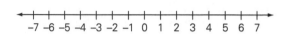

2. $w - 12 > -5$

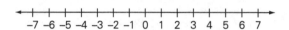

3. $17 \leq 13 + a$

4. $y + 7 \geq 13$

5. $b + 4.5 > -2.6$

6. $h - 1.9 \leq 4.3$

7. $2.5 < t - 5.8$

8. $-9 \geq c - 3.7$

9. $x - \frac{5}{8} < \frac{1}{2}$

10. $y + \frac{1}{3} \geq \frac{5}{6}$

11. $\frac{1}{4} + k > -\frac{2}{5}$

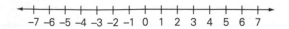

12. $d - \frac{3}{4} \geq \frac{2}{3}$

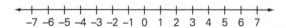

Algebra 1 Rescue! ©2004 Sopris West Educational Services. To order: 800-547-6747. Product Code 169ALG

Posttest

Solve and graph the solution set for each inequality.

1. f + 4 < 7

    ```
    ◄─┼─┼─┼─┼─┼─┼─┼─┼─┼─┼─┼─┼─┼─┼─►
     -7 -6 -5 -4 -3 -2 -1  0  1  2  3  4  5  6  7
    ```

2. y − 6 > −3

    ```
    ◄─┼─┼─┼─┼─┼─┼─┼─┼─┼─┼─┼─┼─┼─┼─►
     -7 -6 -5 -4 -3 -2 -1  0  1  2  3  4  5  6  7
    ```

3. g + 8 ≤ 6

    ```
    ◄─┼─┼─┼─┼─┼─┼─┼─┼─┼─┼─┼─┼─┼─┼─►
     -7 -6 -5 -4 -3 -2 -1  0  1  2  3  4  5  6  7
    ```

4. h − 4 ≥ −9

    ```
    ◄─┼─┼─┼─┼─┼─┼─┼─┼─┼─┼─┼─┼─┼─┼─►
     -7 -6 -5 -4 -3 -2 -1  0  1  2  3  4  5  6  7
    ```

5. x − 4 ≤ 2

    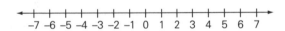

6. z + 5 > 3

    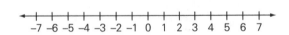

7. a − 4 ≤ −7

8. b − 9 < −8

    ```
    ◄─┼─┼─┼─┼─┼─┼─┼─┼─┼─┼─┼─┼─┼─┼─►
     -7 -6 -5 -4 -3 -2 -1  0  1  2  3  4  5  6  7
    ```

9. n − 3 ≤ −3

    ```
    ◄─┼─┼─┼─┼─┼─┼─┼─┼─┼─┼─┼─┼─┼─┼─►
     -7 -6 -5 -4 -3 -2 -1  0  1  2  3  4  5  6  7
    ```

10. t + 10 > 12

    ```
    ◄─┼─┼─┼─┼─┼─┼─┼─┼─┼─┼─┼─┼─┼─┼─►
     -7 -6 -5 -4 -3 -2 -1  0  1  2  3  4  5  6  7
    ```

Algebra 1 Rescue! ©2004 Sopris West Educational Services. To order: 800-547-6747. Product Code 169ALG

Pretest

Solve and graph the solution set for each inequality.

1. $-2a \leq 14$

$$\begin{array}{ccccccccccccccc} & & & & & & & & & & & & & & \\ \hline -7 & -6 & -5 & -4 & -3 & -2 & -1 & 0 & 1 & 2 & 3 & 4 & 5 & 6 & 7 \end{array}$$

2. $3y > -6$

$$\begin{array}{ccccccccccccccc} & & & & & & & & & & & & & & \\ \hline -7 & -6 & -5 & -4 & -3 & -2 & -1 & 0 & 1 & 2 & 3 & 4 & 5 & 6 & 7 \end{array}$$

3. $\frac{b}{2} \leq -3$

$$\begin{array}{ccccccccccccccc} & & & & & & & & & & & & & & \\ \hline -7 & -6 & -5 & -4 & -3 & -2 & -1 & 0 & 1 & 2 & 3 & 4 & 5 & 6 & 7 \end{array}$$

4. $-3x > -12$

$$\begin{array}{ccccccccccccccc} & & & & & & & & & & & & & & \\ \hline -7 & -6 & -5 & -4 & -3 & -2 & -1 & 0 & 1 & 2 & 3 & 4 & 5 & 6 & 7 \end{array}$$

5. $15 < 3a$

$$\begin{array}{ccccccccccccccc} & & & & & & & & & & & & & & \\ \hline -7 & -6 & -5 & -4 & -3 & -2 & -1 & 0 & 1 & 2 & 3 & 4 & 5 & 6 & 7 \end{array}$$

6. $\frac{y}{3} > -1$

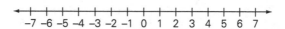

7. $4a \leq -8$

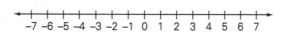

8. $21 < -7z$

$$\begin{array}{ccccccccccccccc} & & & & & & & & & & & & & & \\ \hline -7 & -6 & -5 & -4 & -3 & -2 & -1 & 0 & 1 & 2 & 3 & 4 & 5 & 6 & 7 \end{array}$$

9. $\frac{x}{-3} \geq -2$

$$\begin{array}{ccccccccccccccc} & & & & & & & & & & & & & & \\ \hline -7 & -6 & -5 & -4 & -3 & -2 & -1 & 0 & 1 & 2 & 3 & 4 & 5 & 6 & 7 \end{array}$$

10. $-4a < -16$

$$\begin{array}{ccccccccccccccc} & & & & & & & & & & & & & & \\ \hline -7 & -6 & -5 & -4 & -3 & -2 & -1 & 0 & 1 & 2 & 3 & 4 & 5 & 6 & 7 \end{array}$$

Worksheet 1

Solve and graph the solution for each of the following inequalities.

Example: $\frac{x}{2} \leq -2$

$\frac{x}{2} \cdot 2 \leq -2 \cdot 2$

$x \leq -4$

1. $3x < 18$

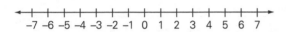

2. $-4y \geq 8$

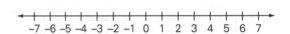

3. $\frac{z}{-3} \leq -5$

4. $\frac{a}{7} > 3$

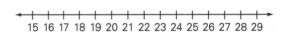

5. $6b > -36$

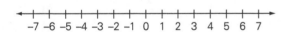

6. $-5c \geq -15$

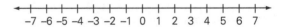

7. $\frac{d}{8} > -1$

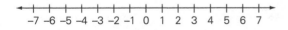

8. $\frac{f}{12} \leq -2$

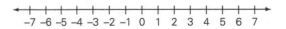

9. $x - 12 < -15$

10. $y + 15 \geq 9$

Worksheet 2

Solve and graph the solution for each of the following inequalities.

Example: $4x < 32$
              $\frac{4x}{4} < \frac{32}{4}$
              $x < 8$

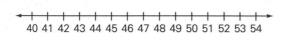

1. $7x < 56$

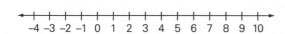

2. $-4y \geq 28$

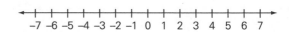

3. $\frac{z}{-6} \leq -8$

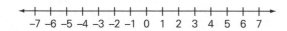

4. $\frac{a}{8} > -4$

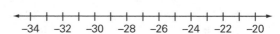

5. $9b > -36$

6. $-5c \geq -75$

7. $\frac{d}{-7} > -9$

8. $\frac{f}{12} \leq -2$

9. $x - 27 < -18$

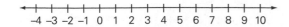

10. $y + 19 \geq 36$

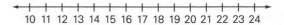

Algebra 1 Rescue! ©2004 Sopris West Educational Services. To order: 800-547-6747. Product Code 169ALG

Posttest

Solve and graph the solution set for each inequality.

1. $7k < -7$

2. $-9a \geq -36$

3. $-3b < 6$

4. $\frac{h}{4} \geq -1$

5. $5y \leq 15$

6. $\frac{x}{2} > 3$

7. $15 < 3a$

8. $\frac{c}{-4} \geq -2$

9. $-7x < 35$

10. $6y \leq 24$

Pretest

Solve and graph the solution set for each inequality.

1. $3x - 8 < 4$

$$\xleftarrow{\hspace{0.3cm}}\overset{\overset{\displaystyle}{\mid}}{}\;\;\text{-7 -6 -5 -4 -3 -2 -1 0 1 2 3 4 5 6 7}\xrightarrow{\hspace{0.3cm}}$$

2. $-4y - 3 \geq -19$

$$\xleftarrow{\hspace{0.3cm}}\;\;\text{-7 -6 -5 -4 -3 -2 -1 0 1 2 3 4 5 6 7}\xrightarrow{\hspace{0.3cm}}$$

3. $2 + 8b \leq -10$

$$\xleftarrow{\hspace{0.3cm}}\;\;\text{-7 -6 -5 -4 -3 -2 -1 0 1 2 3 4 5 6 7}\xrightarrow{\hspace{0.3cm}}$$

4. $-5h - 3 > 2$

$$\xleftarrow{\hspace{0.3cm}}\;\;\text{-7 -6 -5 -4 -3 -2 -1 0 1 2 3 4 5 6 7}\xrightarrow{\hspace{0.3cm}}$$

5. $2x - 4 \leq 6$

$$\xleftarrow{\hspace{0.3cm}}\;\;\text{-7 -6 -5 -4 -3 -2 -1 0 1 2 3 4 5 6 7}\xrightarrow{\hspace{0.3cm}}$$

6. $8y + 10 \geq 26$

$$\xleftarrow{\hspace{0.3cm}}\;\;\text{-7 -6 -5 -4 -3 -2 -1 0 1 2 3 4 5 6 7}\xrightarrow{\hspace{0.3cm}}$$

7. $4a - 7 > 8 - a$

$$\xleftarrow{\hspace{0.3cm}}\;\;\text{-7 -6 -5 -4 -3 -2 -1 0 1 2 3 4 5 6 7}\xrightarrow{\hspace{0.3cm}}$$

8. $2a + 9 < 4a + 7$

$$\xleftarrow{\hspace{0.3cm}}\;\;\text{-7 -6 -5 -4 -3 -2 -1 0 1 2 3 4 5 6 7}\xrightarrow{\hspace{0.3cm}}$$

9. $4 - 5b \geq 9$

$$\xleftarrow{\hspace{0.3cm}}\;\;\text{-7 -6 -5 -4 -3 -2 -1 0 1 2 3 4 5 6 7}\xrightarrow{\hspace{0.3cm}}$$

10. $-2x + 5 > x - 4$

$$\xleftarrow{\hspace{0.3cm}}\;\;\text{-7 -6 -5 -4 -3 -2 -1 0 1 2 3 4 5 6 7}\xrightarrow{\hspace{0.3cm}}$$

Worksheet 1

Solve and graph the solution for each of the following inequalities.

Example: $2x + 3 > 9$

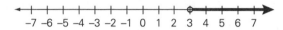

$$(2x + 3) - 3 > 9 - 3$$
$$2x > 6$$
$$\frac{2x}{2} > \frac{6}{2}$$
$$x > 3$$

1. $5x < 20$

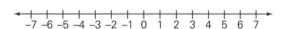

2. $-3x > 15$

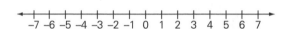

3. $x + 14 \geq 20$

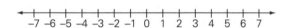

4. $x - 6 \leq 7$

5. $-\frac{1}{2}x > 4$

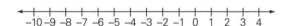

6. $\frac{x}{3} \leq -6$

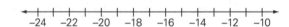

7. $2x + 6 > 16$

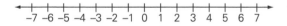

8. $-x + 7 < 3$

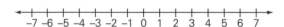

9. $\frac{3}{2}x - 1 > 8$

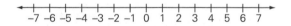

10. $-4x + 6 \leq -2$

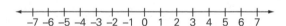

11. $3x - 4 \geq 8$

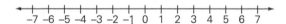

12. $2x - 9 < -13$

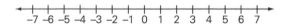

Worksheet 2

Solve and graph the solution for each of the following inequalities.

Example: $2x - 1 > 5 - x$ $3x > 6$

     $(2x - 1) + x > (5 - x) + x$ $\frac{3x}{3} > \frac{6}{3}$

        $3x - 1 > 5$ $x > 2$

     $(3x - 1) + 1 > 5 + 1$

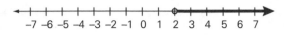

1. $5x - 12 \geq 13$

2. $-8y + 13 < -11$

3. $9z + 25 \leq 7$

4. $16 < 3x + 1$

5. $25 \leq -4y - 7$

6. $19 > 13 - 3z$

7. $2x - 2 \leq x + 7$

8. $3y - 5 > 2y - 9$

9. $z + 15 < 3z + 11$

10. $15 - 3x \geq 2x + 5$

11. $17 - y \leq 2y - 7$

12. $6z + 20 > 4z + 10$

13. $\frac{x}{3} < 2$

14. $\frac{y}{-4} \geq -1$

15. $\frac{2z}{5} > 4$

16. $\frac{x}{2} - 3 \leq 5$

17. $\frac{y}{3} + 5 > 7$

18. $\frac{z}{-5} - 4 < z + 2$

Algebra 1 Rescue! ©2004 Sopris West Educational Services. To order: 800-547-6747. Product Code 169ALG

Worksheet 3

Solve and graph the solution for each of the following inequalities.

Example: $5x - 7 < 3x + 5$ $2x < 12$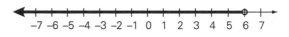
$(5x - 7) - 3x < (3x + 5) - 3x$ $x < 6$
$2x - 7 < 5$
$(2x - 7) + 7 < 5 + 7$

1. $3x + 12 \geq 33$

2. $5y - 13 < 7$

3. $9 - 3z \leq 21$

4. $26 < -3x + 14$

5. $25 \leq 4 - 7y$

6. $19 > 2z + 5$

7. $2x \leq x + 8$

8. $6y + 22 > 8y$

9. $2z + 4 > z + 3$

10. $5 - 3x \geq 2x + 25$

11. $19 - y \leq 2y + 25$

12. $6z + 20 > 3z + 5$

13. $\frac{x}{2} < -4$

14. $\frac{y}{-3} \geq -2$

15. $\frac{-3z}{4} > 2$

16. $\frac{2x}{3} - 4 \leq 0$

17. $\frac{y}{2} + 7 > 5 + y$

18. $\frac{z}{-3} - 2 < -3$

Posttest

Solve and graph the solution set for each inequality.

1. $4y - 9 < 7$

2. $12 - 6a \geq -36$

3. $-30 + 4b \leq 6 + b$

4. $x + 4 > -16 + 5x$

5. $2x - 7 \leq -5$

6. $4y + 10 \geq 18$

7. $3a - 5 > 3 - a$

8. $5y + 11 \leq 4 - 2y$

9. $\frac{x}{-2} < 3$

10. $\frac{a}{3} + 4 < 3$

Algebra 1 Rescue! ©2004 Sopris West Educational Services. To order: 800-547-6747. Product Code 169ALG

Pretest

Solve and graph the solution set for each compound inequality.

1. $x + 12 \leq 25$ or $2x - 38 \geq 2$

   10 11 12 13 14 15 16 17 18 19 20 21 22 23 24

2. $3y - 28 < 20$ and $4y \geq 44$

   5 6 7 8 9 10 11 12 13 14 15 16 17 18 19

3. $|a| \geq 2$

   –7 –6 –5 –4 –3 –2 –1 0 1 2 3 4 5 6 7

4. $|h - 5| < 4$

   –4 –3 –2 –1 0 1 2 3 4 5 6 7 8 9 10

5. $2x - 5 < 13$ and $3x + 4 \leq 16$

   –7 –6 –5 –4 –3 –2 –1 0 1 2 3 4 5 6 7

6. $|y| < 3$

   –7 –6 –5 –4 –3 –2 –1 0 1 2 3 4 5 6 7

7. $4a + 5 \leq 1$ or $6 - a \leq 3$

   –7 –6 –5 –4 –3 –2 –1 0 1 2 3 4 5 6 7

8. $3y - 2 < -8$ and $y + 5 < 6$

   –7 –6 –5 –4 –3 –2 –1 0 1 2 3 4 5 6 7

9. $|x + 3| \geq 2$

   –7 –6 –5 –4 –3 –2 –1 0 1 2 3 4 5 6 7

10. $4x - 3 < 5$ and $3 - 4x < -13$

    –7 –6 –5 –4 –3 –2 –1 0 1 2 3 4 5 6 7

Algebra 1 Rescue! ©2004 Sopris West Educational Services. To order: 800-547-6747. Product Code 169ALG

Worksheet 1

Read each problem carefully and write the answer.

1. A number is less than 7 or greater than 15. Could the number be 11?_____ 17?_____
   6.8?_____ 14.99?_____

2. Name four more numbers that would make problem 1 true. _____
   Name four more numbers that would make problem 1 false. _____

3. Plot, on the number line, all the points that make problem 1 true.

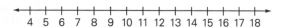

   4 5 6 7 8 9 10 11 12 13 14 15 16 17 18

4. If a number is less than 10 and greater than 4, could it be 7?_____ 15?_____ 10?_____
   5.6?_____ 2?_____

5. Name four more numbers that would make problem 4 true. _____
   Name four more numbers that would make problem 4 false. _____

6. Plot, on the number line, all the points that make problem 4 true.

   –3 –2 –1 0 1 2 3 4 5 6 7 8 9 10

Problem 1 could also be written algebraically as n < 7 or n > 15. Do you see why?
Does n > 15 or n < 7 mean the same thing?_____

7. If n < 3 or n > 9, which of the following would make the compound inequality true?
   Circle the correct answers.

   {–3, 1, 2.7, 3, 5, 8, 9, 9.2, 12, 15}

8. Name four more numbers that would make problem 7 true. _____
   Name four more numbers that would make problem 7 false. _____

9. Plot, on the number line, all the points that make problem 7 true.

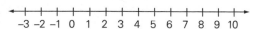

   –3 –2 –1 0 1 2 3 4 5 6 7 8 9 10

Problem 4 could also be written algebraically as y < 10 and y > 4. Do you see why? Does
y > 4 and y < 10 mean the same thing?_____

Algebra 1 Rescue! ©2004 Sopris West Educational Services. To order: 800-547-6747. Product Code 169ALG

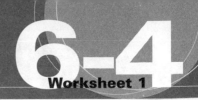

Worksheet 1 (continued)

10. If x < –5 and x > –1, which of the following would make the compound inequality true? Circle the correct answers.

$$\{-10, -7, -5, -4, -3, -1.5, -1.1, -0.7, 0, 2, 5\}$$

11. Name four more numbers that would make problem 10 true. _____
    Name four more numbers that would make problem 10 false._____

12. Plot, on the number line, all the points that make problem 10 true.

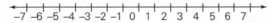

13. If a number is between 10 and 20, could it be 4?_____ 8?_____ 10?_____ 12?_____
    16?_____ 20?_____ 24?_____

14. Name four more numbers that would make problem 13 true. _____
    Name four more numbers that would make problem 13 false._____

15. Plot, on the number line, all the points that make problem 13 true.

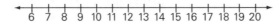

Problem 13 could also be written algebraically as 10 < n < 20, which is read as "10 is less than n and n is less than 20" or "n is between 10 and 20."

Worksheet 2

Solve and graph the given inequality.

1. 3x − 4 < 17

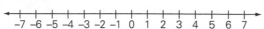

2. 5 − 2x < 1

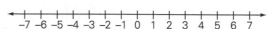

3. 2x + 7 ≤ 13

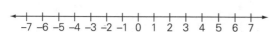

4. 5x − 19 ≥ 16

5. Now consider the compound inequality 3x − 4 < 17 and 5 − 2x ≤ 1.

    The inequality on the left side of the "and" is the same as in problem 1, and the inequality on the right side of the "and" is the same as in problem 2. The solutions to problems 1 and 2 gave easier forms of the solution to the compound inequality. The solution to the inequality in problem 5 is the answers in problems 1 and 2 linked with an "and."

    Write and graph the solution to problem 5.

6. Now consider the compound inequality 2x + 7 ≤ 13 or 5x − 19 ≥ 16.

    The inequality on the left side of the "or" is the same as in problem 3, and the inequality on the right side of the "or" is the same as in problem 4. The solutions to problems 3 and 4 gave easier forms of the solution to the compound inequality. The solution to the inequality in problem 6 is the answers in problems 3 and 4 linked with an "or."

    Write and graph the solution to problem 6.

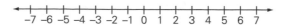

Algebra 1 Rescue! ©2004 Sopris West Educational Services. To order: 800-547-6747. Product Code 169ALG

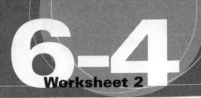

Worksheet 2 (continued)

To solve a compound inequality, we need only to solve each side of the conjunction "and" or "or" and keep the conjunction between them. Solve and graph the following compound inequalities.

7. $x + 5 < 8$ or $-3x < -18$

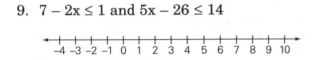

8. $4x - 3 < 17$ and $2x + 9 > 13$

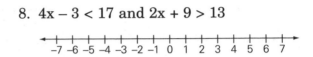

9. $7 - 2x \leq 1$ and $5x - 26 \leq 14$

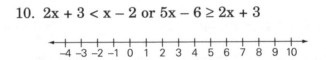

10. $2x + 3 < x - 2$ or $5x - 6 \geq 2x + 3$

Worksheet 3

In problems 1 through 6, draw a line from the compound inequality to the matching graph.

Example: x ≤ 5 and x ≥ 2

1. x < 4 and x > –2

2. x > 4 or x < –2

3. x ≤ 4 and x ≥ –2

4. x > 4 or x ≤ –2

5. x > 4 and x > –2

6. x ≤ 4 or x ≤ –2

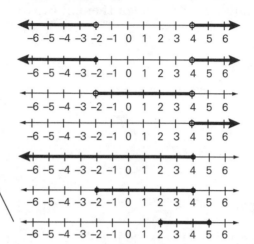

In problems 7 through 12, draw a line from the graph of each compound inequality to the matching inequality.

7. y < 2 and y < –3

8. y ≤ –3 or y ≥ 2

9. y ≥ –3 and y ≥ 2

10. y < 2 or y < –3

11. –3 < y ≤ 2

12. y < –3 or y ≥ 2

Graph each of the following on the number line provided.

13. x < 9 and x ≥ 3

14. y < 2 or y ≥ 7

15. x > –3 or x > –5

16. y ≤ –4 and y ≤ –6

17. x < 8 or x > 4

18. y ≤ 0 and y ≥ 4

Algebra 1 Rescue! ©2004 Sopris West Educational Services. To order: 800-547-6747. Product Code 169ALG

Worksheet 4

Solve and graph each of the following compound inequalities.

Example: 2x − 7 < 1 and 3x + 5 > −1
  (2x − 7) + 7 < 1 + 7 and (3x + 5) − 5 > −1 − 5
    2x < 8 and 3x > −6
    $\frac{2x}{2} < \frac{8}{2}$ and $\frac{3x}{3} > -\frac{6}{3}$
    x < 4 and x > −2

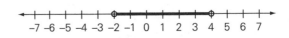

1. 2x − 5 < 1 and 3x > −9

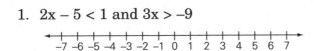

2. 4x − 9 > 7 or 5 − 2x > 7

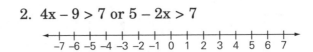

3. 5x ≤ 10 and x + 6 ≥ 4

4. 3x + 4 ≤ 16 or 5x − 9 ≥ 16

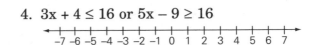

5. −3x ≤ 9 and 4x + 7 < 3

6. 2x − 7 < 5x + 2 or 12 − 2x ≥ 22

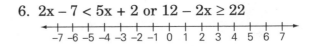

7. $\frac{x}{3}$ ≤ 2 and 5x − 9 ≥ 11

8. 3x − 4 < x + 2 or $\frac{x}{-2}$ + 5 > 4

9. 3x − 7 > 8 − 2x and 14 − x > 3x + 14

10. −3x > 2x + 15 or 4x − 9 ≥ 9 − 2x

Worksheet 5

Solve and graph each of the following absolute value equations and inequalities.

Example: $|x + 2| < 5$

$x + 2 < 5$ and $x + 2 > -5$

$(x + 2) - 2 < 5 - 2$ and $(x + 2) - 2 > -5 - 2$

$x < 3$ and $x > -7$

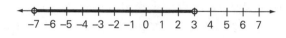

1. $|x - 5| \leq 3$

2. $|x - 3| = 2$

3. $|x - 4| > 1$

4. $|x + 1| = 4$

5. $|x + 2| \geq 2$

6. $|x + 3| < 1$

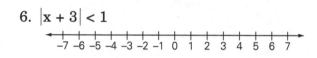

7. $|2x - 5| = 3$

8. $|2x + 6| < 6$

9. $|3x - 9| \geq 6$

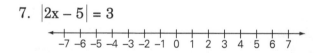

10. $|2x - 3| \leq 4$

Posttest

Solve and graph the solution set for each compound inequality.

1. x – 17 < 8 or 2x – 25 > 37

   +—+—+—+—+—+—+—+—+—+—+—+—+—+—+—+→
   22 23 24 25 26 27 28 29 30 31 32 33 34 35 36

2. 4y – 24 ≤ 28 and 6y ≥ 54

   ←+—+—+—+—+—+—+—+—+—+—+—+—+—+—+→
   7 8 9 10 11 12 13 14 15 16 17 18 19 20 21

3. |a| < 5

   ←+—+—+—+—+—+—+—+—+—+—+—+—+—+—+→
   –7 –6 –5 –4 –3 –2 –1 0 1 2 3 4 5 6 7

4. |h + 3| ≥ 7

   ←+—+—+—+—+—+—+—+—+—+—+—+—+—+—+→
   –10 –9 –8 –7 –6 –5 –4 –3 –2 –1 0 1 2 3 4

5. 3a – 7 < 8 and 6 – 2a < 8

   ←+—+—+—+—+—+—+—+—+—+—+—+—+—+—+→
   –7 –6 –5 –4 –3 –2 –1 0 1 2 3 4 5 6 7

6. 4n – 2 ≥ 10 or 3n + 1 ≤ 10

   ←+—+—+—+—+—+—+—+—+—+—+—+—+—+—+→
   –7 –6 –5 –4 –3 –2 –1 0 1 2 3 4 5 6 7

7. |x| > 4

   ←+—+—+—+—+—+—+—+—+—+—+—+—+—+—+→
   –7 –6 –5 –4 –3 –2 –1 0 1 2 3 4 5 6 7

8. 3a + 5 ≥ 8 or 17 – 1 > 20

   ←+—+—+—+—+—+—+—+—+—+—+—+—+—+—+→
   –7 –6 –5 –4 –3 –2 –1 0 1 2 3 4 5 6 7

9. |y – 2| ≤ 5

   ←+—+—+—+—+—+—+—+—+—+—+—+—+—+—+→
   –7 –6 –5 –4 –3 –2 –1 0 1 2 3 4 5 6 7

10. 4x – 2 < 3x + 7 and 2x + 5 < 4x – 3

   ←+—+—+—+—+—+—+—+—+—+—+—+—+—+—+→
   –4 –3 –2 –1 0 1 2 3 4 5 6 7 8 9 10

Pretest

Pretest

Graph each of the following linear inequalities on the coordinate plane.

1. $y > 3x + 1$

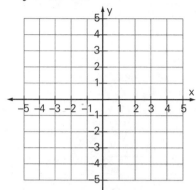

2. $2y - 3x \geq -8$

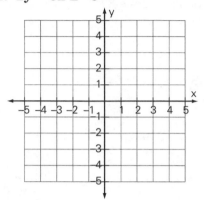

3. $y \geq x + 2$

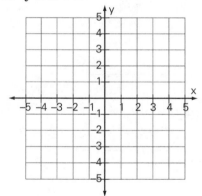

4. $y \geq -3$

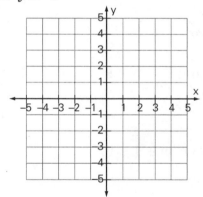

5. $x < 2y$

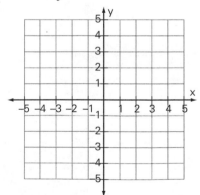

Algebra 1 Rescue! ©2004 Sopris West Educational Services. To order: 800-547-6747. Product Code 169ALG

Worksheet 1

1. Graph the equation y = x – 1.

   a. Plot the point (–1, 2).

   b. Plot the point (3, –1).

   c. For the inequality y ≤ x – 1, which point makes it true, (–1, 2) or (3, –1)?

   d. Shade the part of the graph where y ≤ x – 1 is true.

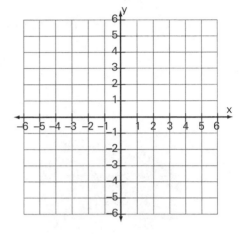

2. Graph the equation y = 3 – x.

   a. Plot the point (–1, 1).

   b. Plot the point (3, 3).

   c. For the inequality y ≥ 3 – x, which point makes it true, (–1, 1) or (3, 3)?

   d. Shade the part of the graph where y ≥ 3 – x is true.

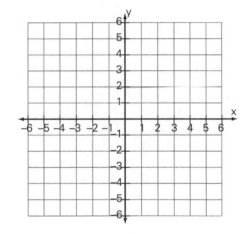

3. Graph the equation x + y = 0.

   a. Plot the point (2, 2).

   b. Plot the point (–2, –2).

   c. For the inequality x + y ≥ 0, which point makes it true, (2, 2) or (–2, –2)?

   d. Shade the part of the graph where x + y ≥ 0 is true.

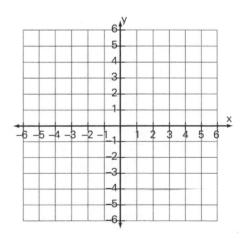

Worksheet 2

Graph each of the following linear inequalities.

Example: 1. $y < x + 2$

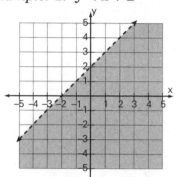

2. $y \geq 2x - 1$

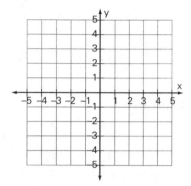

3. $y \leq 4$

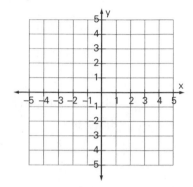

4. $x > -3$

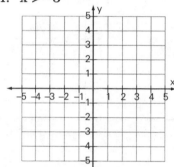

5. $y > 2x + 6$

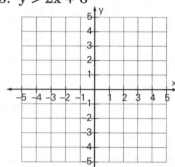

6. $y \leq 4 - x$

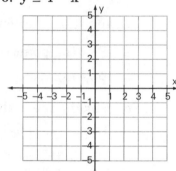

7. $x - y \leq 4$

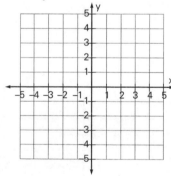

8. $x + y > 2$

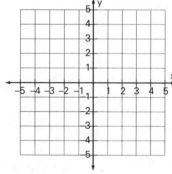

9. $3x + y < -2$

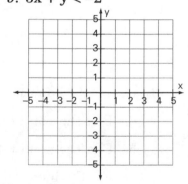

10. $4x - y \geq 3$

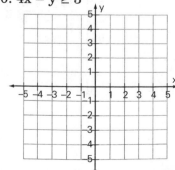

11. $3x \leq 9$

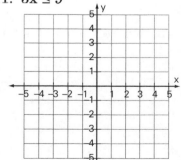

12. $2y > -4$

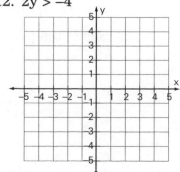

Worksheet 3

Graph each of the following linear inequalities.

Example: 1. $y - x < 2$

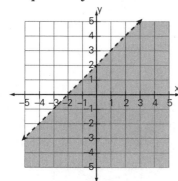

2. $2x - y \geq 1$

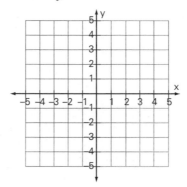

3. $y \leq -2$

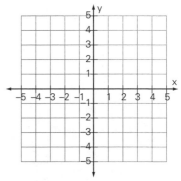

4. $x > 1$

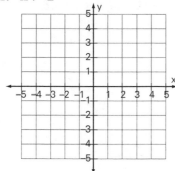

5. $3x - y > 4$

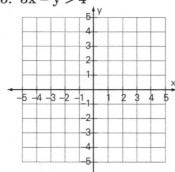

6. $2x + y \leq 3$

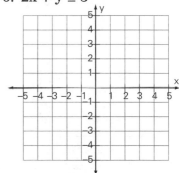

7. $x - 5y \leq 15$

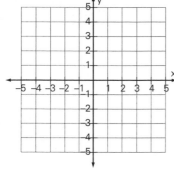

8. $x + 4y > 8$

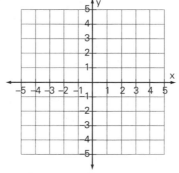

9. $5x + 2y < -2$

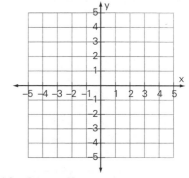

10. $4x - 3y \geq 6$

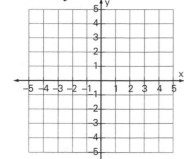

11. $-3y < x + 6$

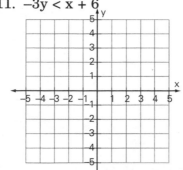

12. $3y > -6$

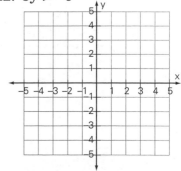

Algebra 1 Rescue! ©2004 Sopris West Educational Services. To order: 800-547-6747. Product Code 169ALG

Posttest

Graph each of the following linear inequalities on the coordinate plane.

1. $y < 4 - 2x$

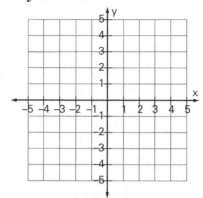

2. $2x - 4y \le 8$

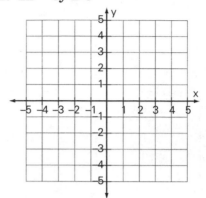

3. $y \le x + 4$

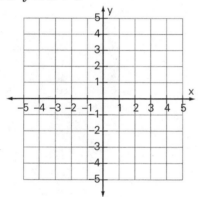

4. $y \le -3$

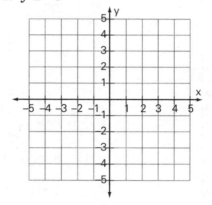

5. $-2y \le x + 8$

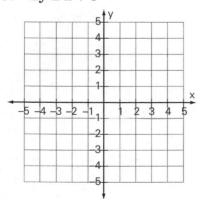

Algebra 1 Rescue! ©2004 Sopris West Educational Services. To order: 800-547-6747. Product Code 169ALG

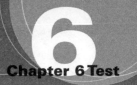

Chapter 6 Test—Solving Linear Inequalities

Objective 6-1

Solve each inequality and graph the solution on the number line provided.

1. $x + 11 < 7$

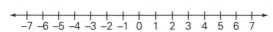

2. $y - 4 \geq -1$

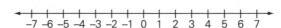

3. $a - 9 \leq -13$

4. $b + 17 > 21$

Objective 6-2

Solve each inequality and graph the solution on the number line provided.

5. $4a < -20$

6. $\frac{x}{3} \geq 2$

7. $-5y < 15$

8. $-3b \leq -12$

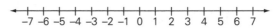

Objective 6-3

Solve each inequality and graph the solution on the number line provided.

9. $4x - 5 > 23$

10. $7 - 2b \leq 1$

11. $2y - 9 \leq -13$

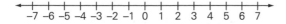

12. $4z - 7 > 7z - 4$

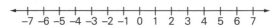

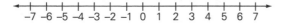

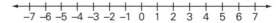

Objective 6-4

Solve each inequality and graph the solution on the number line provided.

13. 3x + 2 < 5 and 2x + 7 > 1

$$\xleftarrow{\ \ }\overset{-7\ -6\ -5\ -4\ -3\ -2\ -1\ \ 0\ \ 1\ \ 2\ \ 3\ \ 4\ \ 5\ \ 6\ \ 7}{\rule{6cm}{0.4pt}}\xrightarrow{\ \ }$$

14. 4y ≥ 20 or 2y − 9 ≤ −13

$$\xleftarrow{\ \ }\overset{-7\ -6\ -5\ -4\ -3\ -2\ -1\ \ 0\ \ 1\ \ 2\ \ 3\ \ 4\ \ 5\ \ 6\ \ 7}{\rule{6cm}{0.4pt}}\xrightarrow{\ \ }$$

15. |a| < 3

$$\xleftarrow{\ \ }\overset{-7\ -6\ -5\ -4\ -3\ -2\ -1\ \ 0\ \ 1\ \ 2\ \ 3\ \ 4\ \ 5\ \ 6\ \ 7}{\rule{6cm}{0.4pt}}\xrightarrow{\ \ }$$

16. |c − 4| ≥ 3

$$\xleftarrow{\ \ }\overset{-7\ -6\ -5\ -4\ -3\ -2\ -1\ \ 0\ \ 1\ \ 2\ \ 3\ \ 4\ \ 5\ \ 6\ \ 7}{\rule{6cm}{0.4pt}}\xrightarrow{\ \ }$$

Objective 6-5

Graph each of the following linear inequalities on the coordinate plane.

17. y > 2x − 3

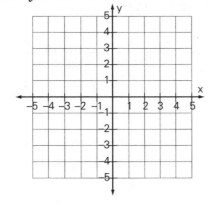

18. y ≤ 1 − 3x

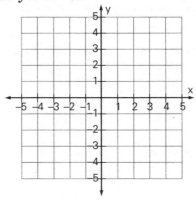

19. x − 2y ≥ 6

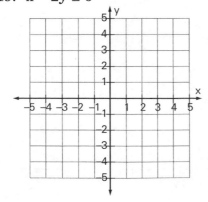

20. x < 4

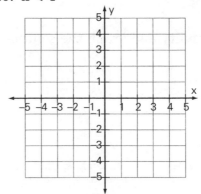

Algebra 1 Rescue! ©2004 Sopris West Educational Services. To order: 800-547-6747. Product Code 169ALG

Glossary

absolute value (| |)   The distance of a number from zero on the number line. Always positive. *Example:* $|-4| = 4$.

associative property of addition   Changing the grouping of addends does not change the sum. *Example:* $(a + b) + c = a + (b + c)$.

associative property of multiplication   Changing the grouping of factors does not change the product. *Example:* $(ab)c = a(bc)$.

axis of symmetry   A line that passes through a figure in such a way that the part of the figure on one side of the line is a mirror reflection of the part on the other side of the line.

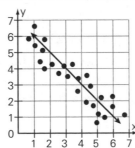

axis of symmetry

best-fit line   The line that will best connect the data or points.

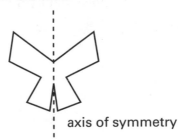

best-fit line

binary operations   Mathematical operation in which two elements are combined to yield a single result. Addition and multiplication are binary operations on the set of real numbers. *Example:* $2 + 3 = 5$.

binomial   An algebraic expression with two unlike terms. *Example:* $3x + 2y$.

coefficient   A number or quantity placed before a variable, which indicates multiplication of that variable. *Example:* 3 in the expression 3x.

commutative property of addition
Changing the order of addends does not change the sum. *Example:* a + b = b + a.

commutative property of multiplication
Changing the order of factors does not change the product. *Example:* a(b) = b(a).

consecutive
In order. *Example:* 8, 9, and 10 are consecutive whole numbers; 2, 4, and 6 are consecutive even numbers.

constant
A quantity assumed to be unchanged throughout a given discussion.

coordinate plane
The plane determined by a horizontal number line, called the x-axis, and a vertical number line, called the y-axis, intersecting at a point called the origin. Each point in the coordinate plane can be specified by an ordered pair of numbers.

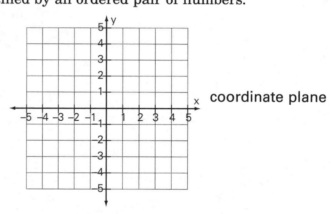

coordinate plane

dependent variables
Two variables in which the value of the first variable affects the value of the second variable.

distributive property of multiplication
For a, b, and c, a(b + c) = ab + ac.

domain
The possible values for x in a function. *Example:* the set of x coordinates in a set of ordered pairs.

equality
A statement that two quantities or mathematical expressions are equal. *Example:* m + 10 = 20 means that m + 10 must have the same value as 20.

equation
A statement that two quantities or mathematical expressions are equal. See also **equality**. *Example:* 3 + 3 = 2 · 3.

equilateral triangle	A triangle whose sides are all the same length.

 equilateral triangle

equivalent	Equal in value. *Example:* 5 + 4 is equivalent to 3 · 3.
evaluate	To ascertain the numerical value of (a function, relation, etc.). *Example:* When you evaluate the expression 3x = y for x = 2; the solution is 6.
exponential	A number written with an exponent. *Example:* 7^{-3}, a^4.
exponential function	Any function in which a variable appears as an exponent and may also appear as a base. *Example:* $y = x^{2x}$.
factor	An integer that divides evenly into another. *Example:* 1, 2, 4, and 8 are factors of 8.
finite	Capable of being completely counted. Does not include zero.
function	A special kind of relation in which every value of x has only one value of y. *Example:* The price of stamps is a function of the number of stamps you buy.
graph	A pictorial device used to show a numerical relationship among two or more things by a number of distinctive dots, lines, bars, etc.
greatest common factor	The largest number that divides into two or more numbers evenly. *Example:* 3 is the greatest common factor of 9 and 12.
horizontal	Parallel to the horizon. *Example:* In a coordinate grid, the x-axis is a horizontal line. ⟵⟶ horizontal line
identity property of addition	A number combined with zero, equals the original number. *Example:* a + 0 = a.
identity property of multiplication	A number multiplied by one, is equal to the original number. *Example:* a · 1 = a.
image	The point or set of points in the range corresponding to a designated point in the domain of a given function.

independent variables	Two variables in which the value of the first variable does not affect the value of the second variable.
inequality	A mathematical sentence that compares two unequal expressions using one of the following symbols: <, >, ≤, or ≥. *Example:* 2 + 3 > 4.
integers	The set of whole numbers and their opposites. *Example:* –2, –1, 0, 1, 2....
integral numbers	The set of whole numbers and their opposites. See also **integers**. *Example:* –2, –1, 0, 1, 2....
inverse operations	Pairs of operations that undo each other and share an inverse relation. *Example:* Addition and subtraction are inverse operations.
isosceles triangle	A triangle that has at least two congruent sides.

isosceles triangle

line (↔)	An infinite set of points forming a straight path that extends forever in two directions.

line

line segment (—)	A part of a line defined as two endpoints and all the points on the line between them.

line segment

linear equation	A first-order equation involving two variables. Its graph is a straight line. *Example:* y = 2x + 1.
mapping	See **function**.
monomial	An algebraic expression with one term. *Example:* 5, 8x and 17mn.
multiplicative inverse	Numbers that multiply to equal one. *Example:* $2 \cdot \frac{1}{2} = 1$.

order of operations	Rules describing what order to use in evaluating expressions. PEMDAS:
	1. Parentheses: evaluate within grouping symbols.
	2. Exponents: do powers or roots.
	3. Multiplication/Division: multiply or divide left to right.
	4. Addition/Subtraction: add or subtract left to right.

ordered pair   A pair of numbers that gives the coordinates of a point on a grid in this order: (horizontal coordinate, vertical coordinate). *Example:* (2, 3).

origin   The intersection of the x- and y-axes in the coordinate plane at (0, 0).

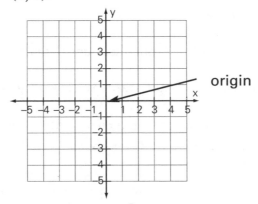

parabola   The graph of a quadratic or second-degree equation. *Example:* The shape resembles the letter U and can face either up, down, left, or right.

parabola

parallel (∥)   Lines that do not intersect; they are always the same distance apart.

parallel lines

perpendicular (⊥) Lines that intersect at right angles.

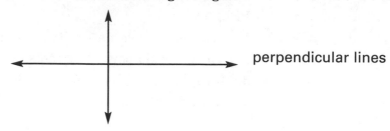

perpendicular lines

point An exact position in space with no length, width, or thickness.

polynomial An algebraic expression with two or more unlike terms. *Example:* 2x + y.

prime number A number that is divisible only by itself and the number one. *Example:* 2, 13.

product The result of multiplication. *Example:* The product of 2 and 3 is 6.

proportion An equation that states that two ratios are equal. *Example:* $\frac{3}{8} = \frac{9}{24}$.

quadrants The four regions on a coordinate plane formed by the intersection of the x-axis and the y-axis.

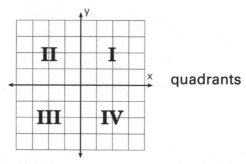

quadrants

quotient The result of division of one quantity by another. *Example:* When 12 is divided by 3, the quotient is 4.

radical ($\sqrt{}$) A symbol that indicates that one is to determine the square root.

radical expression The number (radicand) and the symbol (radical) placed over the number that indicates that one is to determine the square root. *Example:* $2\sqrt{9}$.

range The possible values for y in a function. *Example:* the y-coordinates of a set of ordered pairs.

ratio	A comparison of two numbers, using division. *Example:* $\frac{5 \text{ boys}}{8 \text{ girls}}$.
rational expression	Rational expressions are represented as the quotient of two algebraic expressions. *Example:* $\frac{3x}{6x^2}$.
rational numbers	A number that can be expressed as the ratio of two integers. *Example:* $-\frac{1}{2}$, $\frac{6}{5}$, 0.125.
reciprocal	Two numbers that have a product of one. *Example:* 6 and $\frac{1}{6}$ are reciprocals because $6 \cdot \frac{1}{6} = 1$.
relation	A set of ordered pairs. *Example:* They can be pairs of things (like gloves), or people (like tennis players), or numbers (like 3 and 6).
scalene triangle	A triangle that has no congruent sides.

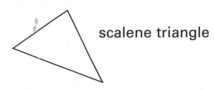

scalene triangle

scatter plot	A graph consisting of points, one for each item being measured. The two coordinates of a point represent the measures of two attributes of each item.

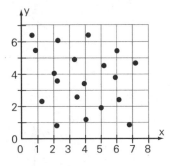

scatter plot

scientific notation	A form of writing numbers as a product of a power of ten and a decimal number greater than or equal to one and less than ten. *Example:* 2,600 is written as 2.6×10^3.
simplify	Combine like terms and apply properties to an expression to make computation easier. *Example:* When you simplify the expression $3x + 4 + 2x + 6 = 40$, you get $5x + 10 = 40$.

slope
The steepness of a line as you look at it from left to right. A line that slants upward has a positive slope, whereas a line that slopes downward has a negative slope. A numerical value for slope is found using two points on the line, where the change in y-value is divided by the change in x-value.

square root ($\sqrt{}$)
One of two equal factors of a given number. *Example:* 5 is a square root of 25 because $5 \cdot 5 = 25$.

sum
The result of addition. *Example:* The sum of 10 and 5 is 15.

symmetrical
Noting two points in a plane such that the line segment joining the points is bisected by an axis. *Example:* Points (1, 1) and (1, −1) are symmetrical with respect to the x-axis.

trinomial
An algebraic expression with three unlike terms.
Example: $3 + t + r^2$.

variable
A letter or symbol used to represent a number. *Example:* In the expression $5y + 2 = 12$, y is a variable that represents 2.

vertex
The point at which two line segments, lines, or rays meet to form an angle. *Example:* $\angle$

vertex

vertical
At right angles to the horizon. *Example:* In a coordinate grid, the y-axis is a vertical line.

vertical line

whole numbers
Any of the numbers 0, 1, 2, 3, 4, 5, and so on.

x-axis	The horizontal axis.
x-coordinate	In an ordered pair, the value that is always written first. *Example:* In (3, 4), 3 is the x-coordinate.
x-intercept	The point where a line intersects the x-axis. *Example:* (3, 0).
y-axis	The vertical axis.
y-coordinate	In an ordered pair, the value that is always written second. *Example:* In (3, 4), 4 is the y-coordinate.
y-intercept	The point where a line intersects the y-axis. *Example:* (0, 4).
zero property of multiplication	When you multiply a number by zero, the result is zero. *Example:* a · 0 = 0.